The Engelking Letters

A Collection of Letters Written by or Pertaining to
Ferdinand Friedrich Engelking 1810-1885

Translated and Edited from the German by
Flora von Roeder

Edited and set by
Stephen A. Engelking

© 2012 Published by Texianer Verlag
Johannesstrasse 12 D-78609 Tuningen Germany
www.texianer.com
Translated by and with Annotations from
Flora von Roeder
© 2012 Flora von Roeder and Stephen A. Engelking
ISBN: 978-3-949197-08-6

*Mrs. Friedrike Engelking, née Niemann,
Mother of Ferdinand and His Siblings*
Photo reproduced from Master of Arts in History Thesis entitled *Texas-Germans' Attitudes Toward Slavery: Biedermeier Sentiments and Class-Consciousness in Austin, Colorado and Fayette Counties* by Cornelia Küffner, University of Houston, Houston, Texas, 1994, p. 56. Original photo was provided by Hinne Goebel of Soest, Germany.

Preface

The book you find before you represents a translation from a collection of letters found in the Detmold, Germany, Archives by Mrs. Anneliese Kastrup of Detmold. Mrs. Kastrup made a typewritten script of the letters from the handwritten collection placed there. The correspondence is dated from 1839 through 1891. Mrs. Kastrup was a descendant of the Engelkings from Schlüsselburg via her descendancy from Ferdinand Engelking's youngest sister, Malwine Engelking Reuter. In the early 1990's, a friend gave me a copy of the typewritten letters he had obtained when visiting relatives in Detmold. Although a novice, I began the long laborious task of translating the correspondence and wrote explanatory notes regarding the communications. The early correspondence was written by Ferdinand Engelking mainly to his mother, but there are also writings to other relatives from the time he boarded the ship in Bremerhaven, which took him to America, until his old age. There is also a letter from his brother during his ill-fated journey to the United States to his mother; diary entries and letters from Engelking's brother-in-law who, with his wife, another Engelking sister, visited the Engelkings in Texas; from Engelking's oldest son to his relatives in Germany; and from his widow, born Caroline von Roeder, to her sister-in-law.

There are a couple of places in the series of letters where there seems to be some missing text. Perhaps a page of the original letter was lost and it was unavailable for the typist. Superscripts in the text coordinate with explanatory notes at the bottom of the pages.

My cousin Stephen (Steve) Engelking of Tuningen, Germany, inherited a copy of the rough translation from his late Aunt Leona Engelking and posted it on the Engelking website. After the 2012 Sack Family USA Reunion, he contacted me and stated that we needed to publish this material before the Engelking Reunion in March 2013 at which time a Texas State Historical Marker will be dedicated at the Engelking Cemetery site designating it as a Texas Historical Cemetery. So the month of November was devoted to overhauling the manuscript, rewriting some of the notes, and communicating via e-mail with Steve as he set the text and designed the cover. We believe you will find in this correspondence a very clear picture of the contrast between what was the comfortable life style Engelking left behind him to pursue his dreams in a raw wilderness on the other side of the ocean.

Flora von Roeder,
Houston, Texas, January 2013.

Contents

THE ENGELKING FAMILY	11
Engelking Father's Accounts	13
Schlüsselburg Sept. 1, 1839	19
To Baumann and Sister Auguste 1839	21
Bremerhaven, Sept. 11, 1839	25
New Orleans, Dec. 24, 1839	27
December 26, 1839	31
Prussian Schlüsselburg, May 31, 1841	37
Notice	43
Wild Cat Spring February 15, 1841	45
February 21, 1841	55
Schlüsselburg January 19, 1842	63
Wild Cat Spring April 24, 1842	65
New Orleans, May 8, 1842	69
September 4, 1842	75
Note June 7, 1842	79
Pecan Grove January 8, 1843	81
Houston April 27, 1843	89
St. Louis, July 2, 1843	91

New Orleans April 20, 1844	97
Galveston, April 23, 1844	103
Pecan Grove June 9, 1844	105
New Orleans January 15, 1849	115
Bremerhaven	117
On Board the FRANZISKA October 3, 1849	117
Galveston, December 22, 1851	123
May 10, 1852	135
Cologne September 11, 1853	139
Schieffer's Residency Application	147
Cologne October 19, 1853	149
Cologne February 7, 1854	153
Cologne June 6, 1854	155
Cologne June 23, 1854	159
Cologne July 6, 1854	161
Cologne August 4, 1854	163
Cologne August 17, 1854	165
Cologne October 7, 1854	167
Cologne November 26, 1854	169
Cologne June 8, 1855	171
Cologne September 19, 1855	175

Bremond June 18, 1870	177
Bremond, Texas June 29, 1870	181
Millheim, Texas January 10, 1887	187
Millheim July 20, 1891	207
Index	209

THE ENGELKING FAMILY

Christian Friedrich Engelking (1759-1830) b. Lahde on the Weser River, Westphalia, Prussia, d. Schlüsselburg, Westphalia; m. Friederike Elisabeth Niemann (1775-1848) b. Schlüsselburg, d. Schlüsselburg.

November 24, 1828
Transcript record of Burgermeister (Mayor) Friedrich Christian Engelking and his wife, Friederike born Niemann of Schlüsselburg:
My children are as follows:
1) Sophie Christine AUGUSTE, born March 14, 1797 (as per LDS website, christened Schlüsselburg), married June 19, 1816, in Lahde, the clergyman Baumann of Lahde.
2) CARL Georg Heinrich, born October 2, 1798, (as per LDS website, christened Schlüsselburg married 5 June 1849, Schlüsselburg, Justine Friederike Auguste Bokelmann).
3) Henriette Friederica Caroline, born Feb. 3, 1801, died July 1, 1806.
4) Christine Charlotte, born Nov. 13, 1802, died May 23, 1806.
5) AMALIE Louise, born Nov. 2, 1804, married at Schlüsselburg Nov. 16, 1828, the Royal Notary, Franz Schieffer of Wegberg.
6) JULIE Marie, born May 23, 1806, married June 30, 1826, in Lahde, 1st Lt. Ernst Bernau.
7) LOUIS Ferdinand, born July 12, 1807, (d. Oct. 8, 1843, bur. Carollton, Louisiana).
8) Friedrich FERDINAND, born Feb. 20, 1810[1]

---

1 Married Ottilie Elizabeth Caroline Louise von Roeder on August 18, 1842, she was the youngest daughter of Lt.

9)   MALVINE Ferdinande Louise, born Dec. 14, 1819,[1] Christened Schlüsselburg, d. 1892, Hagen, m. Judge Wilhelm Reuter (1808-1883) b. Schildesche, d. Höxter, both bur. Höxter.

Ludwig Sigismund Anton von Roeder, founder of Cat Spring, Texas.
1 The church book states she was born in 1820 rather than 1819. She married on Oct. 16, 1838, after this list was compiled, Wilhelm Reuter, Justizrat born in Schildesche, died in Höxter,

Engelking Father's Accounts

For His Two Younger Sons

Schlüsselburg, May 16, 1835:
(Expenses)

Paid out for Ferdinand Engelking	In Gulden[1]	In Cours[2]
Up until the confirmation days no education costs have been calculated. But the following have been calculated:		
1. <u>The cost of the school years</u> of Easter 1824 until Easter 1828 - 4 years at 125 Guilder	500	
2. <u>University years</u> - From Easter 1828 until Easter 1831 are calculated	812,12	400
3. <u>After the university years</u> - From Easter 1831 until the end of December 1832	55	525
From January 1834 until December 1834		422
Total	1367,12	1717

1 Gulden = guilder, a former gold or silver coin of the Netherlands, Germany, or Austria.
2 Cours or C refers to the French word "courant" = the German "Kurant" meaning a coin that was in circulation whose material value equaled its monetary value.

Schlüsselburg, May 16, 1835:

Ferdinand Engelking to further receive		330
1836 and 1837 altogether	120	547
1838		354
1839		220
1839 Sum altogether	1487,12	3168
September 5, for trip to America	800	1487,12
		800
		5672,12

Expenses

	Gulden	Cours
Paid out for Louis Ferdinand Engelking Until his confirmation days, no education costs are calculated. The following, however, are calculated:		
1. The school years from Michaelsfest[1] 1822 until Michaelsfest 1826, 4 years at 125 gulden	500	
2. University years, from Michaelsfest 1826-1827	370	
- ditto - 1827 - Easter 1828	145	
- ditto - Easter 1828 - Michaelsfest 1828	158	
- ditto - Michaelsfest 1828-Easter 1830	547	
3. <u>After the university years</u> From Ester 1830 until end of December 1831	70	470
From January 1832 until 1833 end	270	363
From January 1834 until Dec. 1834 end		300
Sum	2060	1133

---

[1] The feast of the Archangel Michael celebrated on September 29.

Engelking Father's Accounts

Additional statement Schlüsselburg, May 16, 1835
Engelking

Louis Engelking to further receive				331
"	1836	"		332
"	1837	"		338,8
"	1838	"		278,20
"	1839	"	150	153
			2210	2556,4
				4766,4

Mrs. Malvine Engelking Reuter and Husband, Judge Wilhelm Reuter to Whom, of his Siblings, Ferdinand Engelking Felt Closest

Photo reproduced from Master of Arts in History Thesis entitled *Texas-Germans' Attitudes Toward Slavery: Biedermeier Sentiments and Class-Consciousness in Austin, Colorado and Fayette Counties* by Cornelia Küffner, University of Houston, Houston, Texas, 1994, p. 56. Original photo was provided by Hinne Goebel of Soest, Germany.

Schlüsselburg Sept. 1, 1839

Dear Reuter and Malvine,
Don't be surprised that you are just now learning from me that I want to immigrate to America. In decisions which I have already made and which I consider important to carry out, I do not want to encounter contradiction and negative the advice of others who will question my every motive; therefore, you and everyone else will know about this at the same time.
I will sail with 90 other passengers for New Orleans on the Bremer ship, JULIA, on September 6, to become a planter (farmer) in America. Where? Whether in Missouri, Tennessee or another state, will be decided upon after I get there and experience it. I want to farm tobacco and cotton wherever possible. If I am not successful in becoming rich, then I will not be lacking in a small prosperity there. In the worst case, there will be deer and buffalo and other wild game besides the sport hunting animals which will provide food, and for that reason I am taking my double flint rifle and shotgun, my Rhea[1], with me, which I have found to be reliable in

1 Rhea is probably the brand name of the shotgun or rifle to which he refers. Comment by David Griffin, gun expert: "My guess is that this is an obscure maker's name of the Shotgun he carried. It is also possible that he actually named his shotgun "Rhea". Firearms were a valuable and essential part of frontier life and were treasured by their owners. They were often fondly named by their owners. It is interesting that he owned a double flintlock rifle. This is almost certainly a firearm that he brought over with him from Germany. Double rifles were expensive to produce, were usually highly ornamented and were not often the basic hunting tool of a farmer. They have always been fairly uncommon but were more popular in Europe than in

hunting here. If I do well, you can count on deliveries (consignments) of the finest furs and tobacco.

The crossing will cost me as a cabin passenger, including meals at captain's table, 90 Gold; 90 others are between decks--passengers, who only pay 45 Gold. If I can impress enough of these people which I will hand pick, I will attempt the founding of a new colony. I will probably be in New Orleans the end of October and ten or twelve days from there in St. Louis. From there I will write to Mother in detail.

I have remitted to Mother a most exact list of my indebtedness; you will receive it in 14 days to three weeks to satisfy all credits. Of books, which are still in Steinhausen, I want Louis to have the *Manncopf* and the *Decisions of the Geh. of Tribunals*; Carl the *Landrecht and the Gerechts Ordg*; and you dear, Reuter, take the rest for yourself.

Greet all my friends for me, and take a hearty farewell, hopefully not for always, from your brother
Ferdinand Engelking

the U.S."

To Baumann and Sister Auguste 1839

1839

Dear Baumann and Dear Sister Auguste,

On September 6, this year, I will sail from Bremerhaven on the 125 cargo load/250 ton Bremer ship, JULIA, with Capt. Dannemann and 90 passengers to New Orleans. I have reserved cabin passenger status for the purpose of immigrating to America in order to acquire an independent occupation there as a planter (farmer). I have longed for that for years, but now I have overcome the opposition of my mother because she has accepted by fact that I cannot be helped. This is my plan. I will buy in either the state of Missouri or Tennessee a piece of land of about 150 to 200 acres for approximately $250 (300 C^1). My capital is too small to successfully manage a piece of land immediately. I will let that lay for about two years during the so-called "kill-off."[2] This term means that on property with woods, the bark is removed in a circle all the way around bigger trees near the ground. Within a year the trees dry up and after two years they partially fall over due to the wind. The smaller stems (trunks) are then cut down with an ax, whereupon planting of seeds can begin.

During the two years, the value of the land nearly doubles. It will not be so bad during these years to be a manager or accountant or even at worst a fur hunter, whereby I can enlarge my assets about 600 dollars. Then I can energetically begin to manage my own property with an adequate cattle herd and soon develop as an

---

1 See note 2 page 13
2 An American term, which he probably learned from a prospectus.

affluent man. Corn, cotton and tobacco will be the basic products of the soil which I will choose, and if the tobacco is good, you need not have to buy any in the future, dear Baumann. On the other hand, I will furnish Auguste with furs. Do not laugh at these adventurous plans; success will show that I can make them materialize. I will give the most detailed descriptions of everything in my quarterly letters to Mother.

I will busy myself with the exact investigation of the conditions there and their different relationships to each other and well you can imagine that ever more far reaching plans and thoughts are swimming through my fleeting head and it is, therefore, absolutely possible that depending upon the circumstances there, that I may have to deviate from my above-mentioned ideas. Where possible, however, I will bring them to completion.

There is no shortage of wild game there and, therefore, the double flint rifle, and case that I am taking will serve me well when hunting deer, buffalo, etc., especially since I have already become a respectable hunter. To me, such a life appears enviable in comparison to one here where I would become a professional man[1] with 500 C[2] wages in a miserable area with a lot of the type of work that has never pleased me.

Wish me luck on my apparently courageous decisions and bid me a hearty farewell.

Your true brother,

Ferdinand Engelking

---

1 He studied law in Halle.
2 See note 2 page 13.

Bremerhaven, Sept. 11, 1839

Sept. 15
11:15 a.m.
Dear Mother,
Finally, after a long wait, a favorable wind has set in, and I will make use of the few minutes while still on land to inform you that my ship will be out of the harbor in a few moments.
Yesterday evening, our captain and others among whom are Bavarian musicians gave us a brilliant ball with champagne. My captain appears to be a very honest, upright man; his outward appearance inspires much confidence; the JULIA is a new, sturdy ship to which the most excellent sailors belong; and if we should run into a storm or trouble, there is nothing of which to be afraid.
I will probably suffer from seasickness while you read this letter, but if the wind becomes no stronger than it is now, I will probably get by with only a small case of it.
My travel companions in the cabin are a metal worker from Hildesheim of about 35 who earlier amassed considerable wealth in New Orleans and is now traveling there to bring his affairs in order and then return to Germany (he acts like a man of the world, but appears to be an unimportant creature), and a young businessman from Bremen, about 20 years old, who will remain in New Orleans.
Each cabin passenger has his own bunk on which to sleep which is a space about four times as large as my big trunk; it opens out. The between-deck passengers on our ship have it very bad in that respect. They have altogether a space of approximately 28 feet long, 15 feet wide, and 5 feet high; their room is divided by bunks in

squares of 5 to 6 feet and five persons must lie in each bunk, so that each person has approximately 1 foot, 1 inch of space in width.

I exchanged my money in Bremen with very little loss to Spanish doubloons; each doubloon equals 16 Spanish dollars or in local money 20 Gold[1]; you can also imagine how large the pieces are.

I must close and hurry onto the ship and you will receive a further account from New Orleans. Greet Carl for me and my regrets he did not come with me; the harbor is full of ships, about 50, and the Bremer ships are preferable, beautiful from the outside and elegant from inside out; numerous of the cabin furnishings are made of mahogany.

Now take care and wish me a good journey.

Your Ferdinand

---

[1] Illegible in the copy; it appears, however, that he might mean gulden or gold. See note 1 page 13.

New Orleans, Dec. 24, 1839

PR: Feb. 27, 1840
Dear Mother,
You will be surprised that even on Christmas Eve I write to you from New Orleans and that I had not previously fulfilled this duty. I had the bad luck to have had a detailed letter to you and a few other things stolen out of my coat pocket at a local German theater, but fortunately, it contained nothing valuable. Since I intend to leave tomorrow by steamship to Galveston and I still have a lot to do, the above-mentioned loss hurts even more, because I wanted to send you the most detailed news possible, but now there is no time to repeat it.
I will spare you the unpleasantness of an unending 75-day sea journey; our ship arrived here on November 23. I have not ever seen such a magnificent city as New Orleans. Although everyone here complains about the decline in business, there is still a tremendous amount going on. I would lose myself just to write a few pages of description of the goings on. From the advice of a travel companion, I went to a bad hotel, and during the night, because I had forgotten to take my wallet out of my pants pocket and put it under my pillow, a Spanish doubloon (worth 17 dollars here) was stolen. Since different circumstances required me to stay longer, I immediately left there and am staying with Joseph Hahn, a German innkeeper, and for 6 dollars a week, I get proper food, drink, lodging, the best German company in New Orleans.
I had at first a prospect to be a teacher in private hours (tutor) to support myself, but there is an oversupply, so I soon realized New Orleans was no place for me.

Missouri and the remaining Northern United States did not appeal to me because of the cold, so after careful inquiries, I have with great preference decided to go to Texas and become a farmer. Texas is described by many people to whom I talked as a wonderful land, and except for the swampy Southeastern Seacoast, a healthy land. Here for the first time I have heard reliable information from the family von Roeder[1] and my friend Kleberg[2]. Four years ago, the male members of this family fought against the Mexicans and lost all their possessions but have built up a new settlement and now find themselves in a happy, peaceful existence.

A large ownership of land and extensive cattle herds have already made people rich, and through no fault of theirs, grows from year to year. The stream of immigrants is now targeting Galveston, the largest harbor in Texas and 1,200 arrive there weekly. If the value of a morgen of land[3] grows only ½ dollar, Kleberg and his brothers will be about $6,000 richer inasmuch as they have about 12,000 morgen of land in property.

Two of Kleberg's brothers[4] arrived here from Europe a few days ago; we go together to Texas. I favorably purchased tools here, including two plows and a corn mill for a total of $110; I am as adequately equipped as any other farmer; even cowbells and metal milk

1 Von Roeders were founders of Cat Spring and eventually to become Engelking's in-laws.
2 Refers to Robert Justus Kleberg with whom he worked at Petershagen in 1831 and who would also eventually become his brother-in-law.
3 A measurement of land equaling 0.6-0.9 acre.
4 Refers to Ernst and Joseph Kleberg, younger brothers of 13. The former would also eventually marry into the von Roeder family and lived to be an old man. The latter, however, died aboard ship on a return trip to Germany.

New Orleans, Dec. 24, 1839

containers have not been forgotten. The articles are of a beautiful and practical nature; people in Germany have no comprehension of their usefulness. I have among other things an ax with which the felling of trees must be a pleasure.

With my remaining disposable money, I have purchased goods so favorably at the local auction that everyone who knows how to appraise them say that I can sell them in Texas for three times or more what I paid for them. New Orleans is overfilled with European, especially English and French, manufactured goods that at auction here are bought for well under their worth. Naturally, there are also bad and ruined goods among them, but one who uses proper caution can purchase extremely favorable things at these auctions which are held daily. My purchases are for the most part very good. I had a long and costly expense because of my long stay and have to replace it. My dog, which I happily brought with me to sea, was despite all precaution lost in the crowds, and it hurt me very much for the dog was worth 60 to 100 dollars.

December 26, 1839

The steamship which should have departed for Texas yesterday arrived only yesterday unexpectedly and will depart tomorrow. Every immigrant who arrives in Texas before January 1840 receives 320 acres from the government free of charge; he can choose it himself. I came at exactly the right time; the steamship from here to Galveston takes only 48 hours. From there, it takes 12 hours on another steamboat to bring us to Houston, the earlier capital of Texas. Kleberg's farm on Mill Creek,[1] a small tributary of the Brazos in San Felipe County is 58 miles (English, of which 69 equals 15 Prussian post miles) away. This distance we travel by horseback and our belongings will be transported by wagon. I will stay with Kleberg until I have chosen my land, possibly near him, build a small cabin, and plant the first potatoes, which will be ripe in May. It seems strange indeed that I want to undertake setting up my own farm alone. I will in the meantime be caught up in my reclusiveness. The thought that I so purposelessly wasted the last six years pains me. Otherwise, I am full of good spirits and cheerful confidence that I would not change with the most comfortable, most independent job in Europe. For

1 Rising in Washington County north of the von Roeder settlement at Cat Spring, the stream flows south-westward through Austin County and into the Brazos River on the Austin-Waller County Line. The von Roeder grant, however, was a few miles west of the stream although the Lewis Kleberg (another brother who was with the von Roeder and his brother's party) property was located nearer the stream, a bit north east of Cat Spring. He was also a von Roeder in-law. He died at a relatively early age, and his widow then became the wife of Ernst Kleberg.

my complete contentment the only thing missing is living among my relatives. I hope later when settled to give such accounts that anyone in Germany, unsatisfied with his situation, would want to come to Texas to find a better life. As much as this might be in my best interest, I will certainly write the purest truth according to my conviction. Up until now, I hope to get established with the balance of my funds; if this turns out not to be the case, then I hope that you, dear Mother, will give me one last small assistance.

Now as to New Orleans. Of a population of 100,000 inhabitants, there are 10,000 to 12,000 Germans. Although only one-third of the vocations were previously acquired, the waste combined with the greatest greed prevails here, which I have seen in no German city, especially caused by drinking. Although a coffeehouse pays $200 rent annually, one finds here that as much as $500 is paid, so all landlords are becoming prosperous. The houses are in two classes: Bit = gold or 5 class houses, and the Picayune = 2-1/2 class. Every drink, called whatever it is, costs in the first houses 1 bit of which 8 bits makes a dollar; in the latter it costs 1 picayune[1]. In every house is a so-called "bar" behind which the barkeeper stands and serves each drink in only glasses. One goes to such a house, orders a glass of wine, beer, schnapps, drinks it up on the spot, and leaves again, and may in a day in different houses drink 10, 20, 30 or more glasses. Yes, the manual laborer drinks the average of 8-12 glasses a day. An odd custom prevails whereby a

---

1 Picayune: According to the American College Dictionary, colloquially it means something of little value or account, small or petty. However, formerly in Florida, Louisiana, etc., it was a Spanish half real, a coin equal to about six U.S. cents.

complete stranger waves a finger or says "What do you drink?" and would become offended if one refused this without good reason. Many people come together in a coffeehouse at the same time to drink, and every time one pays for all. It is taken for granted that the one who is treated occasionally also treats.

It also makes no difference how scruffy each looks. The baker comes in bare shirt sleeves and covered with meal dust; the bricklayer with the dirt of his craft in the most elegant coffee houses. I used the English word because there is no German coffeehouse; coffee, chocolate, or tea one cannot usually have in such a house; these make little profit and cause too much trouble and Americans avoid the latter.

I must, as all others at my current hotel, clean my own boots and clothing. In the house where I first was, there was not even a chamber pot or a wash basin. The washing took place in a common wash basin which was located in the courtyard with a single hand towel next to it and with which everyone had to freshen up.

As I already said, there are here many Germans, particularly South Germans, many of whom are educated men. Since I have been here, the first German newspaper and even a German theater have started. The former is tolerable; the latter really is bad and will improve in time. The Germans stay somewhat to themselves, and those with whom I have become acquainted are very well behaved people, but there are also many bad ones among them, for whom one might naturally watch out. But among all of them there are bad and good, regardless of what German state they are from and grieve together about the sad situation in their beautiful beloved Fatherland caused by the presence of the arbitrary rule which oppresses every free life style. If someone raises

correct or incorrect reasons for it, they still regard
Germany and its people with compassion.

One eats three meals a day here and the meals always
contain meat. The morning meal contains meat prepared
in different ways, and all three meals are almost the
same. The Americans and the Germans, who have been
here a long time, all eat in unbelievable haste; if one is
called to the dining room and slowly comes in, as we do,
he finds the American already finished; he needs only
two or three minutes, later he hastens again to his shop.
To engage in conversation at the table is unheard of; only
the hands and teeth are continuously working.

My letter would seem somewhat confused in my hurry to
finish because I have personal transactions at the
tollhouse. You must excuse this and its incompleteness;
because of my anxiety I have about the shipment of my
purchases and other belongings, I am in continuous
unrest. Within four weeks, I will write more from Texas.
Since only pre-postaged letters are delivered in Texas,
and that is not done much in Germany, I have made a
deal with my landlord that he will collect all my letters
and forward them to me.

My address is tentatively, word for word:
Über Hamburg via New York
Mstr. F. Engelking
Care of Mstr. J. Hahn Nro 80 Podrastreet
New Orleans

Should any one of my acquaintances have the desire to
come to Texas and have time for me to communicate to
them, have him write to me, and I will write exactly how
to arrange his journey and what to purchase in Germany
and in New Orleans; if anyone has a sum of 800 to 1000
Prussian Talers at his disposal, I can give him
information that will ensure him not only a free trip but

December 26, 1839 33

increase his capital by 50 percent.
Greetings to my loving relatives, all remain well, and more from your loving son next time.
Your loving son,
Ferdinand E.
Have Reuter in the meantime send a greeting to Max from Dr. Decker with the addition that I will write to him later as well. I will be very happy if I can convince him to come here. Hunting animals like bears, tiger cats, wolves, all species of ducks, geese, chickens, snipe, etc., are unlimited.

In another handwriting answered on September 10, 1840, and forwarded to the postoffice at Stolzenau, Friederike Engelking, mother of Ferdinand, wrote down these instructions to Ferdinand's brother, Louis:

Prussian Schlüsselburg, May 31, 1841

As to items of clothing, do not take too much with you. Things you would hardly wear yet in Germany, you can wear here until they are fully worn out. As to the clothing that you usually need are a pair of new grey cloth trousers, you need only about four because they are very expensive to wash; not too light, not too dark, summer trousers are suitable enough. As I did, take many socks with you and up to 18 pair of new strong linen shirts. But in addition to that one or two good wool covers which cost at the most 2 Rp[1]; if you take as much bedding as I did, you will have enough, but in any case, take a longer featherbed instead of a pillow. A pair of jackets of unbleached grey linen would be very good. One seldom needs vests here. In addition to your old boots, bring a pair of new strong cowhide, two pairs of the same type shoes; since these will shrink and dry up, bring them ½ inch longer than usual.

Further, a couple of complete bridles with good bits and bridoons (the local are expensive and bad), one pair of heavy step stirrups with straps, the best is of brass or nickel silver, then a whole skin of good black shiny leather; a good batch of strong hemp rope of differing thicknesses; along with a pair of plow irons; a pair of good braided horsewhips with or without handle; two

1 Rp = an abbreviation of the Swiss coin, Rappen, which is 100th of a Swiss Frank.

(symbol = pfund)¹ boxes of good gunpowder, you can buy a good second-hand gun with flawless Percushions-lock² at a low price, then do it but make sure that it shoots sharp and narrow. I have a bad one myself. Do not buy another gun with Percussion³ unless you can find it very cheap; the local rifles shoot very badly as a rule. One half dozen knives and forks, as well as that many silver tablespoons, also teaspoons, a good set of fire tongs. If you can get cheap good metal bowls (in which to save milk) that hold about 4-6 quarts, about 10 Sgr.⁴ without a lot of trouble, then bring six of those with you; they cost 75 cents to a dollar here; a strong coffee machine; a small lamp; two lights, one scythe, two German spades in good shape and made of good material; and 2-3 pieces of strong cheap calico. These do not have to be of the newest style; the worst costs 37-1/2 cents a yard here. Bring at least 12 pieces of long pipes with you at 10 Sgr.⁵ each, in addition pipe stems and heads; these are unavailable here for any money, and I will soon use up my last pipe.

Of plant seeds, particularly gilly flowers⁶ of all sorts, fruit stones and seeds, don't forget seeds for gooseberry

1. This symbol which somewhat resembles the lower case Greek ω with a line through it stands for Pfund a weight for 500 grams.
2. Percushions = the striking of a percussion cap so as to set off the charge in a firearm.
3. See 2 above.
4. Sgr. = Silbergroschen or one-thirtieth of a Taler, circulating in Prussia from about the year 1821. Current-day Austrian Groschen = 10 German Pfennige or 1 Austrian Schilling. (All to be extinct in 2001 when the Euro became the widely used currency in the European Economic Community.)
5. See 4 above.
6. Plants with clove-scented flowers, such as the clove pink, European wallflower, common stock, or a variety of apple.

Prussian Schlüsselburg, May 31, 1841 37

and currants; particularly Eastern cherry stones, because these cherries I hear do not deteriorate when they are grafted. Bring for me two jackets and two pairs of trousers of yellow nankin[1], a pair of grey cloth trousers, which you can use your size with no problem since we are the same size, a pair of strong cowhide boots and a pair of the same shoes about ½ inch shorter than yours. Do not forget woolen and line yarn, sewing silk, goods, darning and sewing needles. A pair of shoemaker bradawls, and "Sücheln"[2] or "Sielen."[3] A half dozen not-too-small porcelain cups, plates, a sugar dish, a pair of simple capes or hoods, a lot of tar together with hemp yarn for pitch thread, because here one must often work with leather himself. A mortar would not be uncalled for. Also a three-foot iron[4] of which the sides are about 10 inches long, cost here from $2.50-$3.00 some strong sacks, and some wooden spoons (to press butter). I believe the above-named certainly are complete and bring what you can afford without too much trouble and cost to transport, carefully packed. What I have not mentioned, such as a saddle, iron tools, etc., one can

1 A buff-colored durable cloth, originally from China.
2 A notation was made by an Engelking descendant who saved these letters: "According to information from head shoemaker in Soest, "Sücheln" or Süchlen is wrapped around a small awl or bradawl or bore. The "S" is sharply spoken.
3 According to Cassell's Dictionary, a "Sielen" is a towing belt or harness which probably is the same thing as a "Sücheln" or a "Süchlen."
4 This probably refers to an iron tool used for shoe repairs. It was made of cast iron and had three foot-shaped forms to fit different sizes of shoe on a branch around 10 inches long. It was made is such a way that it was always supported by the two feet which were not in use.

advisedly buy here. In the event that you bring along a musket, make a chest that it will just fit into. The one as big as I made in Schlüsselburg (20 cubic feet) is too unwieldy. If, in addition to your luggage and a crate of 12 to 15 cubic feet, you still need room, bring instead several crates of 10 to 12 cubic feet and pack the things equally by weight.

Ernst Kleberg asks if you will bring him one pair of heavy new silver or brass buckle spurs (also bring a pair for me), further, a complete German bridle with spring belt, the bit sharp and of new silver, the leather of the best possible goods. Further, a double bridoon and a couple of stirrups, heavy ones, four or five (Pfund symbol)[1] of new silver or brass.

Finally, Sack[2] asked me to enclose the little letter to his father. Sack requests you to inform his father that in case you come here awhile if you will bring a chest for him, but I tell you here and now that concerning yourself and others property, and specifically the bringing of a crate, involves a lot of trouble. Do whatever you want in this case.

Republic of Texas, Austin County, Wild Cat Spring
February 15, 1841
(Signed) F. Engelking

---

1 The symbol for Pfund, (This symbol which somewhat resembles the lower case Greek ù with a line through it stands for Pfund a weight for 500 grams).

2 Sack is the maiden name of Engelking's future mother-in-law, Caroline (Mrs. Anton Ludwig Sigismund) von Roeder. The person who requested the enclosure is obviously a nephew and his father is one of Mrs. von Roeder's brothers. Engelking writes of the Sacks in several later letters.

The following was written in English. It obviously was a notice that Engelking enclosed in a letter beginning on the next page to his mother to give her an idea of where he was.

Notice

By virtue of an order of the honorable J.H. Moncy, Chief Justice of the County of Austin, I will hold an election at Kleberg's Precinct in Beat Nr 1 at the house of Charles Amsler[1] on the first Monday in February for the purpose of electing:

    one District Clerk
    one County Clerk   for Austin County
    one Sheriff
    one Coroner

    two Justices of the Peace
    one Constable   for Beat No. 1
Wild Cat Spring, January 12, 1841
Robert Kleberg
President offices

---

[1] Charles or Carl Amsler, another settler at Cat Spring in 1834, was of Swiss ethnic background.

Strange Handwriting:

Republic of Texas
Austin County
Wild Cat Spring

Prussian Schlüsselburg
May 31 1841[1]

Wild Cat Spring February 15, 1841

Cherished Mother and Beloved Brothers and Sisters,
Do not attribute it to a lack of interest in you that you have had no further communication from me since my letter to you from New Orleans the end of December 1839; I had already had a letter ready twice, but a variety of circumstances prevented my dispatching them in addition to the uncertainty of correspondence not to mention extraordinary fast changes of all conditions in our young Republic which have an influence on all citizens that it changes from month to month. I would like to place a true picture before your eyes, but it is difficult if not impossible to do on paper. You all would find everything strange and inconceivable; I am at the point of not being surprised by anything.
My health is excellent; I am stronger than I ever have been. Last summer I paid the proper toll due to the weather changes. From May until August except for a few short periods I had the hot yellow fever from which almost every new arrival is sick. I got a worse case than usual. I felt symptoms of being unusually tired and I probably have the help of a good doctor and the careful care of the earlier referred to Robert Kleberg and his

1   This is possibly the handwriting and date of the recipient of the letter, which is approximately 3½ months after it was written.

good wife, Rosa von Roeder[1], to thank for my recovery. I will now try to describe as briefly and coherently as possible my life and work since my departure from New Orleans. On December 29, 1839, I went on a steamship in the company of the brothers Ernst and Joseph Kleberg and their companion Neuton (earlier Nathan), which anchored on December 31 on the shipyard of Galveston, where we got off the next day. At this main port of Texas, where wooden platforms grow out of earth daily like mushrooms, we traveled on a smaller steamship on January 2 and arrived on the morning of January 3 at Houston. Earlier the seat of government, and as was Galveston founded in 1837, it is the main place for the land transactions of Texas. Both places appear to be odd to the new arrivals from Europe.[2]

***

(Note: There is some portion of this letter missing, but from the text that exists, Engelking is describing Texas horses.)

They are descended from the Andalusian "Race"[3] in Spain but are very degenerated, fairly small, very durable, but mostly malicious. They have the valuable quality that on trips, they can make the 40 miles without having to eat all day; they are satisfied if they can feed on grass overnight. That they still have high-born

1 Wife of Robert Justus Kleberg and Engelking's future sister-in-law.
2 The description of this part of the trip ends abruptly with this page. There appear to be some missing pages; however, the text of the next portion appears to correspond with the writer newly arriving in Texas and describing how things are done or his impressions of what all he sees and experiences in this place.
3 Using the English term, he refers to the small, wild Spanish horses that roamed through the Southwest.

Wild Cat Spring February 15, 1841

bloodlines is revealed in their use as breed mares. If they are mated with good American stallions, they bring the most beautiful colts for which they could be used as racehorses. The Mexicans bring them in great numbers into the country and sell them wild (unbroken, that is, not yet ridden) for $5 each; as soon as they become tame enough to be led by a rope, depending on the different quality, they cost $10-$20; if they allow themselves to be ridden, they are worth $15-$30. If one only wants to use them as breed mares, he buys them only as rope gentle and their colts from good American stallions are worth after three years from $50-$100 and more; on the other hand the offspring from a good stallion is $8-15.

One gets also mules from them, but the offspring of a good donkey stallion is likewise very expensive. A good donkey stallion costs more than $100; on the other hand, one can let the mare run with the stud more; whereas a finer stud one must feed in a stall. A good mule sells very easily, especially in the United States.

Here, one eats three meals a day, always warm, mainly meat, and drinks with it coffee or tea. The bacon for breakfast, as you would no doubt think, is very good tasting and a healthy treat. I read recently in the translation of the ODDYSSEY by Vohs[1], and had to laugh that the splendid swineherd, as he treated his King Odysseus, had also found this out. By the way, the bacon here and pork in general is better tasting than in Europe; the reason is the pigs are allowed to roam freely and eat the lovely foodstuff of acorns, walnuts, and wonderful pecan nuts which lay in bushel fulls under the trees.

One gets up before sun-up and goes to bed again early in the evening so that no one has the opportunity to enjoy a

---

1 Assumed to be the translator of the Greek into German. The author of the Odyssey was the Greek Homer.

glass of wine in the public houses to lengthen the evening. Recreation here in the manner of that in Germany is seldom. Hunting and cattle-driving (both on horses) provide the merriest of parties and contribute to conservation of energy and much health. Actually, to me, to drive the wild beef cattle to the house is the greatest amusement. The beast runs where it can and seeks to evade the riders in all possible ways to escape into the most impenetrable "Bottoms"[1] (thickest on the riverbanks). The course goes many miles through hill and valley forest and bush, whereby the rider seeks to cut off the beast from the thickest woods and bottoms.
Therefore, one must often make turns in full run. It is a beautiful view to see four or six riders in full gallop drive the herds of cattle or breed mares into the pen on the farm.
If one wants to feed the animal at a specific area of his pasture, he starts a fire in that area of the prairie. One needs only to throw a coal in the long, dry grass, and it catches fire instantly and burns rapidly or slowly, depending on the strength of the blowing wind. If one wants to clear a small bit of prairie, perhaps 500 acres, he sets it on fire towards evening, and the fire dies down with the heavy dues of night. In Germany, one cannot have such a splendid show at night as a prairie fire. Depending on the weather after such a burning, in 8 to 14 days, three weeks at the longest, there appears a covering of the most beautiful young grass, and there the animal grazes. As soon as this bit of grass goes bad, a new section of the prairie is burned away, and so it goes all year long. It is regrettable that often the fires spread through the woods and many trees are killed and others stunted in growth, but because of the surplus of wood,

1 Other American terms.

this damage is slightly regarded.
The character of the Americans has, despite many good qualities, some sides that are not so pleasant. At the top are arrogance, smugness, and over selfishness. They regard themselves as the Jews during the time of their magnificence as the chosen people of God, and the Anglo-Saxon race stands out as an example before all other nations. They regard the German in general as dumb, because it is not difficult for them to shamefully cheat a trusting new arrival from Germany out of something. So they understand how to persuade, especially the new arrivals, to purchase land that is not valuable, portraying beautiful rivers, brooks, woodlands, etc., which do not exist or are not worth talking about. So are home sites in towns which do not exist offered for sale. There are no pre-drawn plans of these towns showing the public places, buildings, railroads, etc. Such proposed cities are in places where there is nothing to find but prairie and number in Texas about 50 with names like Aurora, Tuscaloosa, City of Brazos, etc. On the other hand, it is absolutely true that some cities originate from pre-drawn plans and these are slowing building up but the mischief in such land, cities, and railroad speculation is on all accounts large.
Pity the unfortunate German newcomer who is not familiar with the English language and has not been able soon after his arrival to take the advice of some stranger (and here one must use more than usual discretion), and, unfortunately, I must add that his own countrymen who immigrated earlier do not always act to the benefit of the new arrivals, but they calculate to their own advantage. The newcomer does well to suppose this, at least until he is convinced to the contrary.
A commendable exception to this is the farmer Ernst of

Industry[1], 16 English miles from here on Mill Creek; he assists his newly arriving German countrymen with advice in an extremely unselfish manner. Also in the city of Houston, there are about 100 Germans living there, who are united into a Society[2] under the chairmanship of the respected merchants Fischer and Danzwert[3], who advise the helpless German newcomers, and if necessary, provide them with assistance and see that they are not deceived with fraudulent land titles. German newcomers, for that reason, would do well to get advice from these people because the law which promised every immigrant 320 acres free of charge, in the beginning was only to be valid until January 6, 1840, and has certainly been extended by this year's Congress for an unspecified time, but inside the settled areas, most of the good land is almost all cultivated by its owner (many landowners have over 100,000 acres). There are also in the cultivated areas land owners who will joyfully give several hundred acres to a family with the only condition that they settle on the land. The immigrant must have the county

1   Friedrich Ernst took possession on a league of land in Northwestern Austin County in the spring of 1831. In 1838, he established there the first post office west of Galveston, built a boarding house, and began a cigar production business. Known as Industry, the town is historically referred to as the first German settlement in Texas.
2   The first German Society in Texas or the "Deutscher Verein für Texas." It was joined by 53 of the 75 males who lived in Houston at the time.
3   Henry Francis Fischer or Fisher, commissioned as Consul for Texas, went to Bremen with a letter of introduction from Count Boos-Waldeck to Count Castell, general manager of the Adelsverein. Fisher informed Castell that 6,000 families could be settled on a tract of land located in the Texas Hill Country. At the time, it was inhabited by Comanche Indians.

surveyor measure out seven acres, naturally at his own expense. He does well to see this as a small advantage, since he can settle there when the rush towards the West has been secured. In the not yet settled areas, because of danger from the Indians for many other reasons, settlement is unfeasible; almost every newcomer who wants to farm is required to buy as much land as he thinks necessary from the large landowners.

But all this takes me too far off the subject; in order to be more clear, I would have to go into an extensive explanation. I will therefore prefer to return to my own affairs. As I finished my business with Kleberg last year, I had the intention to set up a small farm that same autumn. Since I did not want to cook my own food, it was necessary for the execution of my plan to buy the necessary land near a farmer where I could buy my food. So I got into negotiations with the Swiss Amsler which fell apart because he thought too much of his land. This was the same case with Roeders and Kleberg. For $2.00 per acre I could have indeed bought 100 acres, but in my position, this was a too oppressing task, and I had to give it up temporarily. I was sorry for this for the following circumstances. Last spring I had bought some white Italian mulberry seeds of which I obtained 1000 tree shoots, which in the fall were already 3-6 feet high. Not to mention that these trees are very valuable as shade trees due to their fast growth and thick leaves (I sell them as such for $1.00 per dozen) so that in a few years when the silk cultivation in the fall comes here, as it already has in the Southern states of North American, an incalculable profit could be expected.

Transplanting too often must naturally be obstructive for growing trees, but since they were so close together, it was necessary for me to transplant them this winter on leased land from where I will have to move them as soon as I have my own farm. Furthermore, I like complete independence with no strings attached, and through the knowledge of being one's own master over his property and the petty inconveniences that are caused by living alone, to feel sufficiently compensated. Perhaps I can be partners with a German my age named Hollien[1], who worked here on Roeders' farm, and who stands out through his reliability, diligence, and circumspection, can with him build a suitable place next fall.

My financial position is as follows:

Cash monies	$3
An outstanding debt, in return for which I am required to take cattle	140
An American workhorse	60
A Spanish riding horse	15
2 cows with calves	26
3 brood sows, 2 year-old bores (males hogs), the young sucking pig not included	28
On farm tools	50
On miscellaneous articles that I got from splitting up the business as cotton shirts, covers, etc.	60-80
Remaining different articles other than clothing, underwear & bedding	50

1 This letter from Engelking, dated February 1841 in which he mentions Hollien as a potential partner, indicates that the latter was single like Engelking himself. He was. He returned to Germany a couple of years later and returned with a wife. According to The Cat Spring Story, published by the Cat Spring Agricultural Society in 1956, Johann (Hans) Hollien and Hulda Ramm were married in Rostock, Mecklenburg, on March 21 1844, a son was born to them in Galveston on December 6, 1845, after which they came by ox-wagon to Cat Spring where they settled among the other German settlers.

$432

The result is nothing less than magnificent; if I would have had the experience last year that I have now, it would have turned out even different; also I hope to substantially improve my circumstances yet this year. Dear Mother, I would like for you to send me another 100 Lsdor[1] if I know of a completely safe opportunity to improve my future, but how to safely send the money here? I see no way, so I will just continue to scrape by. My personal upkeep is ok and with time, it will be somewhat better.

---

1 Lsdor = Louis d'or another form of currency in Europe similar in name and value to Danish, Hanoverian, and Dutch currencies. All worth just under $4.00.

February 21, 1841

Dear Mother,

I received your letter of September 9 last year, day before yesterday. How great my joy over that was, you can hardly imagine. I noticed that not a single line whatsoever from my relatives was enclosed. I conclude that you still enjoy your excellent health and that you considered it superfluous to speak of it. I learned from Sack that Baumann is out of danger. He and his wife (This would be newlyweds, Philip and Theodore Ploeger Sack) were here the beginning of December last year. The rest of the news of our family is exceptionally joyful with the exception of Louis'[1] health. I would have at least expected that Louis did not completely pass his third Relations exam[2]. I do not see this small misfortune as a failure; his poor health and the bad attitude that comes from that, as I am in complete agreement with you, is the main misfortune. If these evils are not lifted, he will never be able to hold a public office with this lifestyle without completely ruining his health. If he has any inclination to come here, as I almost conclude near the end of your letter, and he must really embrace the decision after sufficient reflection, I can only wish him luck. I believe with some confidence that change of climate, lifestyle, and sea voyage would have a positive effect on his body. I ask you, dear Louis, to consider

---

1   Louis Engelking, immediately elder brother of Ferdinand.
2   Relations exam may refer to some aspect of Louis' profession, possibly law. Earlier in his first letter to his brother-in-law, Reuter, Ferdinand expresses how he wishes his books, all obviously related to his own legal studies, divided, and Louis is a recipient of some of them.

whether you feel you can forsake all the small comforts of German life for the raucous unpleasantness.

If you could bring 1500 C[1] gold (almost 1200 local money) cash with you for both of us, we could together set up a very lovely farm, buy plenty of cattle, and hire a Negress or a white woman to do the housework and have the hardest tasks done by day laborers. You will not be overwhelmed with work. In case you should come over, I am writing on the enclosed paper the most appropriate things to bring with you.

Inquire about the best medicine for seasickness and take it. I suffered only insignificant bouts, but it could be worse for you. In the beginning of September or perhaps earlier, you can begin reading notices in the Bremen newspapers of the ships going from Bremen to Galveston, noting those that go direct. It saves much cost, a lot of fuss, and stops. I would advise you to travel only in the cabin. Do not arrange for a ship in advance through a broker but travel with a pass. Try this from Bremerhaven where you have the best chance and from where many ships depart close together. Cautiously, inquire as to the character of the ships' captains (with this you will surely have trouble getting the truth) and choose the captain and ship you like best. Since the ships depart a few days after what is announced in the newspaper, you need not be in Bremerhaven before the announced departure. Do not let anyone notice, especially in America, that you have a substantial amount of money on you. You will understand enough English so that you can do this in a makeshift manner and for sure you will know enough by your arrival in America. Bring no other books except what you absolutely cannot do without for your reading; I have English grammar and dictionary

1   See note 2 page 13.

here.
When you arrive in New Orleans, the captain will take you with him to the customs house where you will have to swear that your effects belong to you and are not for sale in America. Then obtain permission to bring your articles on land and then it is best to go to the innkeeper, J. Hahn, at No. 80 Poidras Street; he is a sensible, honest man to ask advice if you need it, and he perhaps could help you. Embark on the next steamboat from New Orleans to Galveston. The passage costs, I believe, exactly as when I came here $30 in the cabin and $12 on the covered deck. Because the trip only lasts 36 to 48 hours, I chose the covered deck and had to provide my own food which I brought from New Orleans for that reason. If I were you, I would also choose the covered deck, and should you run into unreasonable weather, something like rain and north wind, then under way, explain to the captain in person that you would like to pay for the cabin. The weather in the winter season in the Gulf of Mexico, which I discovered for myself with a great deal of displeasure, is occasionally very turbulent. In Galveston, you need to deal with the customshouse the same as in New Orleans. I know no one there who can help you in case of trouble; however, Baumgarten from Stolzenau lives there, whose brother in Stolzenau perhaps would give you a letter to take with you. It is best for you to travel in the cabin from Galveston to Houston. In Houston, go to the merchant Dankenwerth and let him keep your trunk and crates until they can be sent from there by ox cart. It is best for you to buy at the daily auctions in Houston a Spanish horse and, if possible, with a saddle and bridle for $10 or $15 total; if more than $25, do not buy in any case. Do not consider making the trip from Houston to here on foot. You would

regret it and save nothing by that.

I have forgotten to tell you that you would make the best exchange of Bremen German money in Columbian or Mexican or possibly Spanish doubloons. Of the first two, one pays $15 in Bremen and the last $16; the first ones are worth here every bit of $16, the last $16.50-$16.75. Exchange into North American gold pieces has the smallest advantage. However, do not be persuaded to exchange your good money into Texas money or other paper money in New Orleans, Galveston, or Houston. Besides the damage you could incur if the value of this money drops, you run the risk of getting counterfeit bills. I have given you this information in great detail because of my experience. In case circumstances have changed since then, then use your own judgment.

If you believe that you cannot do without your dearest Rhine wine on your sea journey, take some with you. I believe you will indeed do it, but you will not be able to keep from treating the captain and some cabin passengers on the trip.

Now a short answer to your letter, dear Mother. That Hartmann wants to continue torturing himself in Germany makes me feel sorry for a man like him. If he brought his wife and about 1200-1500 C[1], he soon would enjoy more comfortable property, and certainly his children would be better off. Poverty only happens here due to ones own fault. Max Von Der Decken, as I know him, would do very well here without any capital. I would take him in with open arms. The odd lack of cash money here, I assume, is caused by the fact that money is suddenly being amassed in Europe. It cannot help but happen when things are right that real estate will go up in price., and consider it very prudent that the value of the

---

1   See note 2 page 13.

February 21, 1841

Hecker Farm[1] is at a high price.
If Louis comes over, I consider it as most advantageous if you will negotiate the amount of money that you will give him through a loan in Bremen. Or if you can do this through a dependable reasonable man, you can get the money for a mortgage of 2-1/2 to at most 3 percent. You come out much better than if you cashed secured capital which pays a higher interest rate. In Bremen, there are many businessmen who will lend against a mortgage at the above-mentioned interest rate.
The piece of linen which you gave to me I sold to Robert Kleberg; he offered me $12 for it, but I would not take more than $10. In general, linen is hard to sell here; the American prefers to eat and sleep in cotton cloth. No name lives with his wife, who is expecting to deliver a child in four weeks, in a small house rented from Robert Kleberg. They have brought only a little money but know how to get by here very well, and since the man seems to be very industrious and cautious, then I don't doubt that their future looks very good. Probably Otto and Albrecht von Roeder[2] would donate some land where they will erect their own farm in the next autumn. To get married here is as such an improvement of one's wealth, but I doubt that I will ever be able to make that decision. What I will acquire as far as wealth, I will probably leave to one or the other nephew who might have the desire to come to live with me in Texas. But those are things that we do not talk about yet. In any event, I will return to Germany to visit you all in a few years. I will possibly

---

1 Perhaps a family property in Germany. This is the only mention of it.
2 Engelking's future brothers-in-law.

bring a load of Texas Kanaster[1] and cigars which are equal in quality to Havana cigars with me. Tobacco cultivation will indeed remain my principal occupation. If Louis wants to come here, write me this immediately and I can begin an arrangement for it. I know of two pretty places to farm, one 9 and another 12 miles west from here on roads to Austin, one of which I would buy. I believe letters to me now would be fastest and safest at the following address:
    Via Havre
    Mr. F. Engelking
    Wild Cat Spring
    Texas
    Austin County
Now dear Mother, take care and be not troubled about
Your loving loyal son,
Ferdinand Engelking
Give greetings to all of my relatives, also Hermann von Möller. Greet all of my old friends in Halle through Reuter, and tell the good assessor Velhegen in Halle that as soon as I have the opportunity, I want to send him a case of cigars from my own factory; so that he won't be able to smoke his bad 4-pfennig[2] cigars again. Also, I send you greetings again from Robert Kleberg.

---

1 A colloquial German word for tobacco.
2 Pfennig = the coins of Prussia. After World War II, the Reichmark was changed to Deutschmark or Mark with 100 Pfennigs = 1 Mark until 16 Dec. 1995, when the Euro was introduced into the European Community and is the currency of 17 countries including Germany.

The following was obviously a receipt for a letter posted by Friedrike Engelking to her son:
On 22 July 1841 on Ferdinand Engelking wrote and ps. paid 1 Rp. 12 Sgr
Herr Rend. Engelking

1841 July 23	1 letter for America		
	1 3/16 lts.	1 M	12 Sgr.
Windheim	Kgl Post Expediteur Hitzmann		

Schlüsselburg January 19, 1842

To Banker Levisohn in Minden
The merchant Mr. Delius of Versmold has relayed to his brothers in New Orleans my request to transmit to my son F. Engelking in Texas an exchange of approximately 500[1] And will charge the withdrawal to me.
In my good name, thence, I wish by this means to inform you of this and at your earliest convenience to acknowledge to me the receipt of this by my son, and I pledge to make good this amount.
Obediently yours,
Wilhelm Engelking
Burgermeister

---

1   Unknown. Monetary term was not included in typewritten draft.

Republic of Texas, Austin County

Wild Cat Spring April 24, 1842

Dear Mother,
Over a year has elapsed since I last wrote, and you have not complained about my tardiness. Twice I started a letter to you, but the interruption of unforeseen events did not allow me to finish. I had intended to come to Germany in February but, because of several adversities, especially the devaluation of the Texas paper money, I was unable to get together the necessary money for the trip.
Since my last writing in February a year ago, I received letters the beginning of August from Baumann and an enclosure from Julien, the beginning of January from you, the next one received was Amalien's, and finally in February, I received one from merchant Delius in Versmold with the information of your order to him to place a deposit for me of $400 through the commercial house of Schmidt and Corp. In New Orleans. This motherly care, which although I would not solicit, and which should outfit my needs, I acknowledge with childlike gratitude.
I will now tell you how things have gone with me during this time. On March 15 of last year after I had just leased a field, I came down with an intermittent fever, not exactly dangerous, which lasted until the middle of May and prevented all work. When my strength returned again, planting time was over with. With great effort, I obtained some 2,000 tobacco plants, whereof I harvested some 500 pounds of tobacco. As a result of two months of neglect, my corn yielded only a half crop. I traded my only horse for sheep, which are seldom expensive to

raise and extraordinarily profitable, but dogs I had never seen, attacked them and tore them to pieces; the remainder fled into the woods, and I could not find them again. Such misfortunes have not beaten me, in that the return of my health has given me strength of body and cheerfulness of spirit. In August when I received Baumann's and Julien's letters, my resolve from your support as in Deutschland ripened, and if need be I would ask my brother-in-law, Schieffer, for a small loan. I had seen that being fully alone among strangers could not be for me, and at last had myself a girl and resolved that of all importance, I make her my wife. The girl was poor as I, and without support from Germany, I could not think of providing for a marriage, and yet I was old enough and did not want to wait for better prospects.

The difficulty is to obtain the necessary travel money; horses, cows, and things like that sell for very little cash money, although the row of tobacco that bears cigars would. I resolved, therefore, to make cigars for the market and to go to Houston. I had estimated in February the project would have brought altogether some $150. My plan failed, and I had to make a decision to tentatively remain here. Hardly had I on February 1 arrived from Houston back in Cat Spring, when to my greatest joy, I received the notice from Delius that he had placed on deposit for me per your instructions $400 at Schmidt and Company in New Orleans. I wrote immediately to Schmidt and Company that I wished the money transferred to a good bank in Houston; fell in love with Caroline von Roeder, the 18-year-old daughter of our patriot here, bought me a beautiful piece of land, made a contract on account with a builder for the necessary structure, and made all the preparations to be married soon.

Wild Cat Spring April 24, 1842

Suddenly on March 7, we were notified through a messenger of the news that a supposed significant Mexican army was making a forward thrust on the city of San Antonio/Bexar on the occupied west border some 200 English miles from us, would take us over, and volunteers were needed to rush to the scene. The same day, we brought home our best horses on the prairie, set our muskets, got our riding clothes, provided ourselves with food, and rode early on the following morning toward the threatened area. There were our five Germans from Cat Spring; our troop increased itself fast by which, from all sides, riders came rushing to the scene with their supplies without orders from any authority or officers, but each on his own incentive, something commonly used here. Four days after we were on the so-called scene, the Mexicans, the number amounting only 800 to 1000 men, had two days earlier, fallen back from San Antonio to the unoccupied prairies of the West, and would not strike again. When our supplies began to play out, we turned back home, this quite useless activity having cost us more than 14 days.

When we were long back home situated in freedom, we saw groups of riders coming from the outlying regions of West Texas next to that taken over, who drew the universal opinion (from a reported approximately 80,000 souls) of a cry for revenge against the Mexicans and the Government now, and the talk is that we must push forward to the capital of Mexico and take it before full freedom will come. I am very calm in the face of all these outcries, for I do not believe that a serious, decisive war will come between the Mexicans and Texans, for both sides are too weak and divided to arm themselves. If one reads the full accounts of the American newspapers, many imagine themselves to hold the facts and all the ideas.

When I arrived back home at Cat Spring from this small deviation, I began the development of my new farm, which lays on Mill Creek four miles from Cat Spring. It was nearly three months since I'd written and not had an answer from Schmidt and Co., and the lack of money hindered me in outfitting, and I decided to go to New Orleans myself; a merchant there who had befriended me had already loaned me the necessary travel money. The cost of the trip is not freely insignificant, but I am compelled to accept this offer. I will write more to you from New Orleans and want to depart the day after tomorrow.

New Orleans, May 8, 1842

Schmidt and Co. had not received my letter, thus their silence. They prepared to pay the $400 not in silver but only in banknotes. Delius' writing to Schmidt of the $400 was for Spanish taler. The difference in interest between silver and bank notes is substantial; silver now has 6 percent premiums. I, therefore, lost $24. If you will instruct Herr Delius not to forget to reimburse the worth of $400.

Again, dear Mother, I say to you my heartiest thanks for this unexpected help. I will now marry in from 2 to 3 months. My bride is a strong, healthy girl, in spirit and mind, which in Texas shows in all the work which is expected in the wife of a farmer. I do not doubt that I will have a happy life with her.

I have bought from Louis Kleberg, with a promissory note for $120, due to be paid early next year, a piece of superior land of 177 acres. I bought a very good and spacious house, which was already largely completed, for $140 from a German in Cat Spring, having paid $80 direct and $60 due early next year; it will cost around $200 to be completed but will be the best and most spacious house in the whole surrounding area. It is of four corner square timbers, which exactly pass each other, 18 feet in the square. The main room, a bedroom, is 10 feet broad and 18 feet long on one side, off the other side is a gallery (shade roof) (American porch) with a roof of 10 by 18 feet. I was lucky to buy and have the adjacent buildings moved from an abandoned farm not far away for a ridiculous price. I needed only to pull them down and drag them to my place. I have kept my best horse; I have bought a yoke of oxen for $46. I now have 18 head of cattle, including 6 milk cows with their calves. As soon as I get back to Cat Spring, I want to buy six additional good cows and calves. Because my pigs were fed quite incorrectly for two years, I only have 4. A harvest of sorts in the coming summer is not possible; the development of my farm will take my whole time. Early in the next year, after enclosing the fields and reclamation of the land, it will be ready. I will never attempt a large amount of cultivation; corn for my needs and some tobacco for sale will be my main products. My intent is mainly to be a stock raiser, tentatively beef stock, which brings roughly 40 percent capital interest. Should I be able to acquire a herd of some hundred sheep, I would be very lucky. The profit from that is over 100 percent, the wool not included. One counts on a mother sheep (ewe) to have three young in 2 years. Now, dear Mother, I have a great request of you. Allowing for some comforts around me (although not of the European concept), I still need $400. I have projected that if you would send me yet $400, I will pay off my land and my house early next year totaling $180, which I have contracted. The recently received $400 goes for the detailed estimates for the limited domestic and farm equipment. My bride, of course, has a right of $400 Prussian Cour for a dowery out of the Sack Family Foundation in Silesia[1]; this money is but far away yet. I have a notarial record of our engagement, another of which my prospective father-in-law has and which will be sent to the Sack Foundation. As soon as my wedding

---

1 As a daughter of Caroline Luise Sack von Roeder, Caroline (Lina) von Roeder was entitled to a dowry upon her marriage to Engelking from the trust fund endowed by Simon Heinrich Sack in 1792 for the progeny of his nieces and nephews. Caroline Luise Sack von Roeder was one of those nieces.

occurs, the marriage certificate will be sent. The local foundation will be notified that my brother-in-law, Reuter, is the nominated authority to carry these documents.

Should my brother-in-law, Schieffer, loan me from his profits over 3 or 4 years around $1000, it would be of significant help. I can offer him no certainty, and I say casually that only in the severest need, such as those as the result of my previous struggles, could I become a bad credit risk; Schieffer certainly has no doubts about my validity.

There now is an established Bremen business office in Galveston, Texas, under the name of Kaufmann et Comp, and through the Bremen office of J.A. Graeser, you will receive this letter. I believe also, that this is a safer way for sending correspondence between us. Should Delius consign future moneys to me, it would be best for me through the above-mentioned office with a directive for it to be in silver.

Since my previous letter from Cat Spring, no one in the surrounding area has died, and many children have been born. Theodore Sack[1] had a girl in March last year, and in April this year, a second; Rosa Kleberg bore, after three previous daughters, finally a son last year in

1 Theodore Sack, born Ploeger, was the wife of Philipp Sack. First cousins, the couple married in Germany and immediately embarked for Texas to where their Aunt Caroline Luise Sack von Roeder lived. In a letter from one of Ferdinand Engelking's close friends, Amanda Fallier von Rosenberg, and published in a translation of those letters, it is revealed that Engelking and Theodore Ploeger had been engaged when both still lived in Europe. One wonders if his great desire to leave Europe stemmed from his wanting to get away from the outcome of this failed relationship.

October. Louise Kleberg and Caroline von Roeder (born Ernst), widowed from Louis von Roeder, since last summer married again with Albrecht von Roeder) look forward daily towards their confinements. The storm of well being is flourishing in Cat Spring. Last summer, a theologian Ervenberg from Herford immigrated here from Illinois, where he had been a preacher. Twelve children, who up to now were yet heathen, the oldest of whom was 6 years old, were baptized all at once.

I had believed my stay here in New Orleans would last longer, and I would undertake the answering of Baumann's, Julien's, and Amalien's letters, but the time will be too short here; perhaps I will have some time in Galveston to write them a few lines if I have the opportunity. I learned that the departure of the boat upon which I will return to Galveston has been delayed a half day; thus I make use of the time to write to you, dear Mother. You must excuse my writing which is very confused, for my head is full from remembering all the directions given me by others to take care of their purchases from the many shops.

The anger, which momentarily dominates North America entirely, will naturally be very disadvantageous to Texas. Hardly no one in Europe has an idea of the money shortage here. Texas has but itself to blame for the most part. The consumption of imported products and commodities through only the slightest authorization is up to now unbelievably great. Only in the past few years have things begun to work such as exporting a quantity of cotton. Now, the beautiful land is beginning to take shape. The old fields are being enlarged and better tilled, showing the results of active hard work. The seasons this year were so extraordinarily favorable that one can with certainty look forward to the richest harvest. The export

New Orleans, May 8, 1842

of cotton in the previous year was considerably up proportionately, and this year will increase more than twice, and Texas will soon establish affluence.
The necessities of the farmers are most negligible. Meat, vegetables, and things like that he grows himself. Clothing is very low priced, and because of the mild climate, it needs to be only very lightweight. The main expenses of the already outfitted farmer are for sugar and coffee, the latter of which is very good, strong and drunk often three or four times a day. Delivery prices are almost nothing.
I have such a free, unconstrained life here that I would find it difficult to get used to European activity again. I would like to make a trip to visit you, which for the moment is undoable; whether I can at some other time, I will have to see. It pains me very much that Louis' health is not yet better. I do not believe that he will be content in Germany, but it is doubtful that he would come here. Should he come, I would give him a most brotherly reception. Now, dear Mother, I ask for your blessing for my approaching marriage and for whatever help you can give me. Greetings to my brothers and sisters.
Your son,
Ferdinand Engelking

September 4, 1842

Dear Mother,
Hopefully, you long ago received my last letter, which I sent through a Bremen ship's captain. I have been afraid that a letter from you is lost. Your letter with the postmark "Windheim" of July 23, 1841, I received last winter, but have received nothing further since that time. I can confidently assume that you would have reported to me the remittance of the $400 to New Orleans. In the meantime since then, no letter from you has arrived.
Since August 16, I have been the lucky husband married to Caroline von Roeder. Since that time, I have lived here on my own farm. The absence of a home and sharing with others which I have always appreciated, I have missed, and particularly in the last year has often awakened a melancholy feeling. That is now over, and I look forward to a peacefully serene and contented future. A better wife I could not have, especially for life in Texas.
My farm is located five English miles from Cat Spring in the direction of San Felipe in a very lovely region with rich land, good woods and water, and a lovely house. My house is one of the best and most spacious in the whole area. This fall, I will build a second kitchen and particularly a smokehouse. I hope to make ready a small field early in the next year.
The first arrangements of the house construction and the purchase of 177 acres have, as you can imagine, cost a large amount and have put me $250 in debt, with many things yet needed in the household, which I regretfully let my wife do without. For this reason, I once again ask if it is in anyway possible to send $400. The bearer of

this letter, Joseph Kleberg, who wants to return here from Germany towards the end of January, is reliable enough to entrust with what you want to send me. Could you also send the articles which I asked Louis to bring with him if he came here, in that they would not take up much room and not cost much to send. Should Louis still decide to come here, he now has a good opportunity with Joseph Kleberg; he would be very welcome to be with my wife and me and could with very little money and reasonable endeavor have an independent life here.

My livestock now consists of roughly 30 head of cattle, and pending no bad luck, will increase next year to 45 to 50 head. Also shortly, I will have a lovely young mare which I bought for $5. My next goal is to enclose 15 to 20 acres and to buy about 50 head of sheep.

I have received one letter from you completely by chance that did not go through the innkeeper Hahn in New Orleans, and have worried about it. Therefore, address future letters to me to him. I hope that the bad ink will not be unreadable if you receive this letter; I can come up with no better momentarily. Joseph Kleberg has surprised me as to his journey and waits on the closure of this letter. He has promised me to personally visit you in Schlüsselburg to relate all to you from me that he knows. He will take residence in Paderborn, so have Baumann, Auguste, and Julie, to whom I unfortunately do not have time to write, take this good opportunity to get together with him.

Now, dear Mother, take care and greet all brothers and sisters from
Your true son,
Ferdinand Engelking
P.S. My dear wife heartily greets you.

Note June 7, 1842

Handwriting of Friederike Engelking born Niemann, mother of Ferdinand

    Mr. F. Engelking
    Wild Cat Spring
    Republic Texas - Austin County
    c/o Mr. J. Hahn
    Post Office Industry
    Nr. 80 Poydras Street
    New Orleans

For F. Engelking in Texas written and forwarded to the postoffice in Stolzenau, and postage paid as far as Bremen   3 M^1 9 gr.

        Schlüsselburg, June 7, 1842
        Engelking

A trunk with items of clothing and similar things with horse regalia   to F. Engelking to Dr. Baumgarten at Stolzenau for the dispatch to his brother, Merchant Baumgarten at Bremen, forwarded on Sept. 6, 1842.

---

[1] This might be an abbreviation for mark or Reichmark.

Pecan Grove January 8, 1843

Beloved Mother,
My last letter to you and my siblings was luckily carried to you by Joseph Kleberg from Galveston on September 22; I hope that a letter I dispatched last May by means of the Bremen house, Kaufmann and Co. reached you. Your letter of June 6 last year I just received in October, and I take the opportunity to reply to it now.
The Counts from Waldeck and Leiningen-Westerburg of Nassau have been in Texas almost three months touring on immigration matters, and the latter, who appears to be an excellent and trustworthy young man, will return to Germany via New Orleans and the United States; he has promised to carry this letter.
First I will answer your letter point for point. The trunk of which you wrote that Ploegers sent out and one in which Auguste enclosed dispersed things for me, has not arrived. Sack, to be sure, in March last year through the merchant Dankwerth did receive a trunk with similar contents indeed dispatched by his father, and contained nothing for me. I have learned nothing of Baumgarten until now, and it sounds that if you entrusted money for me, which would be dear and beneficial; it is not there. I have received the $400 through Schmidt & Co. In New Orleans and also through Joseph Kleberg. You comment that I could not need doubled sums; I need to assure you not to be negative.
I am very sorry that Louis will not come here, and I sincerely hope that it is in his best interest and makes you happy. Reuter's children are coming rapidly, but Germany offers them such an uncertain future that their father must feel a certain sorrow. Should I, as I hope, be

blessed with children, I can confidently expect that they will have it better than I. That Julie after her separation from Bernau will experience happier days, I am confident. But for their children, particularly Arnold and Ernst, Germany offers no favorable future, so it would be very reasonable to learn a good handcraft, especially room and cabinet building, and try their luck here. I would be like a father to them, and they would have an insured independent life. I would be all the more happier if they or one of them would come earlier. They need not wait so long as to be self-supporting enough to make the trip alone; from time to time one finds convenient opportunities to travel with someone.

Letters I have up to now received from you include one from September 1840, which I received in February 1841 and immediately answered, one from Baumann, Julien, and Amalien, one which the applicant, Saul, took with him and which was forwarded to me through Hahn in New Orleans which I received in August 1841, and sent the answer to these in September 1841, with Joseph Kleberg; your letter of July 21, 1841, I received in January 1842 and answered in May last year from Galveston. The Bremen House of Kaufmann and Co. forwarded this letter to Graeser & Co. in Bremen for sending on. Finally, your last letter I received in October. Joseph Kleberg has taken with him a letter for you and one for Baumann, in which I had written enclosures for Louis, Julien, and Amalien.

Should the trunk you mentioned in your last letter not yet have been sent out or not gone with Joseph Kleberg or a better opportunity, it would be best to ship it through Graeser & Co. in Bremen to Kaufmann & Co. in Galveston. Whichever is most practical based on your own knowledge and the content of my earlier letters

Pecan Grove January 8, 1843

through Joseph Kleberg, you may encumber the trunk. I never dreamed that I could be so happy as I now am. The matrimonial and domestic luck I now share at the side of a darling and loving wife more than compensates for the previous loneliness in which I lived. My wife is a model of good management and hard work, and I could not, especially for life here, make a happier choice. I always must tell her of you and my siblings. My happiness will double towards the end of summer when she will make me a father.

At present, I am still incapable of paying many unusual debts, so we live quite alone on our farm and do our separate jobs. Tables, chairs, cupboards, bedsteads, and such things I have made all myself and have no furniture in my house that I have not made. My furniture is so unlike yours that one would never think how I earlier despised such work, but of course which I now tolerate. My home is set on sandy ground near where a spring flows; within a range of 200 paces lies the most fruitful land, so that I can make my field near enough to the house. A fruit-bearing garden immediate to the house which is convenient to the first "kuhpence"[1] is already built; every cultivated ground must have a half foot of the fattest "kuhdüngers"[2] to fertilize it. So this year, I can cultivate approximately two acres at the house immediately through my cattle to raise the most fruitful crop. An individual like me earlier, whom as you know, was not the most industrious, naturally cannot prepare very much land. Other chores and domestic transactions

---

1 Cow pens
2 Dung shows no plural and no umlaut in Cassell's, MacMillian Publishing, New York, c 1978, but it seems logical to guess from the above that Engelking is fertilizing his garden with cow manure from his cow pens.

are so numerous that not much spare time remains for jobs outside the house.

I want to make this clear to you. I have 32 head of cattle and a yoke of oxen of which the owners buy up differently. Because the dry "prairie-grase" has no taste in the winter, we move the cattle to the "bottoms" to the most narrow valleys, small creeks, and brooks where woods and ground vegetation and endless green grass grow. Every head of cattle goes back there in the winter and seeks nourishment until February or March when the green prairie comes out. It costs much time and effort to round up the scattered cattle from all points by horseback to home, sometimes fruitlessly seeking them out, as you can think.

I have among my cattle 15 cows which will have calves, and each cow requires the least time to drive up using horseback; now and then one does not find them and other times, the cow is not willing to be driven home, but seeks to escape in the bottoms with the calves, in which case, good dogs perform excellent service in which case the horse does not. I think that in this year with a second house to complete and, in addition the garden by the house, planting ½ acre of tobacco will be enough drudgery and have no desire to use any more of my time on that.

A money shortage which no one can remember reigns now in Texas as in all of North America. Only low production of goods on the market sells. Cows are only valued at $8 to $10 per head, and I believe they could fall lower, and only producing cattle with discretion, as mentioned above, can one be profitable in beef cattle. Cotton is 6 cents and tobacco has fallen to 10-12 cents per pound, and these compete freely with low-priced European-manufactured products from England, France,

and Bremen.
The Mexicans attempted an invasion again in Texas this past fall, for some reason to take away San Antonio. They were turned back after rapidly advancing through the next regions of residents, and as I with my neighbors wanted to directly engage them on September 30, we received the news of their complete withdrawal status. The young Mexicans' desire for war has been apparent ever since a small army reached 600 or 700 united men on their own territory. This undertaking appears so silly with a trifling quantity of troops with deficient discipline, and is but a rubber band, especially in recognition of our republic by defiant and feeble factions of Mexico. It is momentarily recalled that when they crossed north of the Rio Grande, our side lost 30 people with 400 Mexicans killed and 1200 captured[1]. If this report is true, it is certain they exaggerate their ability. Mexico is too powerless and the Mexican soldiers too bad, in my opinion, to be hazardous to Texas, but Texans err as an average about the importance of Mexicans wanting to bring this single territory into line. Although the government of Texas is literally without money and therefore without strength, life here, is to be sure, of deepest freedom, if neither war with Mexico nor confusion and murder which is not unusual in these young times can be reckoned with and not disturb the peaceful citizens.
Auguste Ploeger, whom you mentioned in your letter via Baumgarten wanted to come here to her relatives, will, with impatience expect more from a young German man at Cat Spring than she thinks. Deaths in Cat Spring have

1 He may be referring to various skirmishes preceding the Mexican War between the U.S. and Mexico after Texas became a state in the union.

for a long time not been as frequent, and one hears of more births, and the young children grow healthy and strong. A schoolhouse was built the previous summer, and one looks for competent teachers, as the three oldest children are seven years old.

The money I asked you about in both of my last letters is hopefully already under way. After receipt of this, I will be on a footing to pay my debts for the house and purchase of land, organize the house and make the land productive which is still in a deplorable state, and buy some milk cows and sheep. Apart from that, you already know I have bought two horses, and my wife's brother, Otto von Roeder, gifted my wife with a riding horse for which she has no use because she has no ladies' riding saddle. To purchase such, which costs at most $20, I have not yet been able to do. A slide which my horse or my oxen must drag forth laboriously on the ground up to now is my only means of transport; I would like the pleasure of a wagon, because with the slide, riding the fence rail with every piece weighing between 50 and 100 pounds to make a good enclosure, requires having to make 7000-8000 drives, and goes fully too slowly. Because of a shortage of cash, I must tentatively do as well as I can.

I am, thank God, with my wife, healthy and strong, as I hope that you and all of mine are also over there. My wife greets you heartily. I hope to receive a letter from you soon and could write you again soon. Now take care.
Your true loving son,
Ferdinand Engelking

Do not forget to address letters to me with the address Post Office Industry. The name, Pecan Grove, is not yet known; I have just now given it to my farm because of the many pecan nut trees that grow around here.

Pecan Grove January 8, 1843

Baumann and Auguste, Schieffer and Amalie, Julie with her children, Reuter and Malvine, Louis and Carl are all brotherly greeted from me.

Houston April 27, 1843

Dear Mother,
I have let lie, waiting on a suitable opportunity to send the enclosed the old letter, in that Leiningen took another way and did not pass by here. Three weeks and 14 days ago, I received both letters from Reuter, besides the first and second exchange of $400 of Schmidt and Co., in New Orleans as I had asked you. I thank you for your generosity.
My wife is looking forward toward the end of her confinement, so I lost little time making the arrangement so I could make the trip to New Orleans and return the middle of May. The excellent care and accuracy with which Reuter provided the exchange has made it possible for me to exchange the entire amount at a local merchant named Shackelford. I saved through that an unpleasant, costly, and time-consuming trip and will ride home yet today where tomorrow evening I will quite unexpectedly be by the side of my wife.
Reuter refers in his first letter to a letter from you which I have not received, to my and my wife's greatest regret; we had already long in advance received your next letter. I am happy only that from Reuter's letter, your health is excellent.
Joseph Kleberg, I have learned, died en route on the trip from Galveston to Liverpool. Other letters, which had gone with him to Germany, have already been received here, so I hope that all mine are there.
I am extremely happy, so happy, as I had not believed I would or could be in this life. I as well as my wife are healthy; our burdens are smaller from day to day through my work as through your motherly love. I have now,

young and old together, calculated between 50 and 60 head of beef cattle and think that this year will increase to 80 yet; my pig breeding will bloom; chickens swarm by me.

Ernst Kleberg, who saw Baumgarten a short time ago in Galveston, told me that you wanted to give Baumgarten nearly $1200 for me; I have explained to Baumgarten, however, that this is just a misconception. Also asked that should a trunk for me have arrived in New Orleans, would I a written arrival procure.

I am in a hurry and can not write more to you; in general, the times in Texas are very bad; money is not in the country and products such as cotton, tobacco, sugar, hides, and others have farthest lower prices.

Take care and stay healthy.

Your true son,

Ferdinand Engelking

July 3, 1843, letters from Ferd. Engelking of January 8 and April 27, 1843, at Pecan Grove, received here on July 31 sent to Reuter at Paderborn. Both letters of January 8 and April 27, 1843, were attached and returned here.

Engelking

A single letter from Louis Engelking, Pr. Schlüsselburg, August 17, 1843 (strange handwriting, perhaps of the mother).

St. Louis, July 2, 1843

Dear Mother,
As I predicted, the old inborn ailment, which has let up at no time up to now, caused much unspeakable pain on the entire trip. Subsequently, aboard ship (it departed April 17), first black coffee, then water or nothing to drink with oat soup were fruitless, but I found if taken with black coffee, helped most, but in no way enough. I had taken no wine with me, because it (preferably Mosel or light Rhine, of course) was too expensive in Bremen!. I would prefer not to think back on this trip and to only mention that after an eight-week voyage during which there was no real storm that rocked or roared peril, the ship luckily arrived in New Orleans with crew and passengers. Of the latter, 50 were in-between decks, and eight with me in the cabin, namely, 1) a tool dealer, Hicks, from Germany returning to his New Orleans established shops; 2) a medical doctor, Drews, from Dessau, who, after making exams in New Orleans wanted to practice; however, his expectations have declined since his arrival; 3) a young American, Hermann, who had returned to his parents in New Orleans from Bremen, where he attended to business; 4) a young Hanoverian from the area of Verden, Tewes, who wants to enter his uncle's business in St. Louis as a business clerk; 5) a Jewish comic from Vienna, who wants to take up farming near his relatives in the neighborhood of St. Louis; 6) his wife; 7) their three

children; 8) Heymann from Triest, companion of the comic.

The merchant, Schmidt, in New Orleans, by which I made every exchange and asked about transportation said there might be nothing but an only steamship departing in about 14 days and not returning again and not to anticipate there being other ships available to that place. (I had taken with me every bar on the recommendation from Heye) and on which I had Heye to write a separate letter of recommendation for my further dispatch to Texas in order to avoid circumstances that could cause me trouble in other respects because of shortages and each association with Texas. At that time, the heat already reigned and was for me a circumstance that seized my body, and I was exhausted, and it had not yet reached its highest degree. (In general, a very intense fever was predicted for this year.) It appeared to be quite unreasonable for me to remain in an adverse location as is New Orleans, where it is expensive, hot, and unhealthy, where the hottest time yet awaited me and wait to set out on a trip with perhaps many delays again. One can only be secure in the summer time with the yellow fever unless he goes north. St. Louis is north of New Orleans on the Mississippi, the first great region where I was secure, as it is less hot and unhealthy (yellow fever has never gotten here) and where it is also much cheaper than New Orleans. On this basis, I, in the company of the above-mentioned Tewes, came here (on one of the many steamships of which a few depart daily). The eight-day trip (it is 1200 English miles or 300 German miles) has cost me, including the transportation of my trunk (round 2 dollars), not more than 14 dollars altogether. My stay over time in New Orleans would cost me not much less.

St. Louis, July 2, 1843

I have found room and board here in the United Hotel for 5C[1] weekly; subsequently suitable and an inexpensive accommodation for my useless circumstances. The first thing after my arrival, it was necessary to write to Ferdinand, and as soon as the first letter was sent, I repeated it, because I wanted it to be safe. I neglected to denote the innkeeper Dankenwerth as Consignee (recipient) which would provide for forwarding. I have explained to Ferdinand that circumstances proved (I have been advised by speaking more German) it would be best first to get used to the hot climate if I remain here until the autumn comes here and that he can determine the time that he can meet me coming from New Orleans or Galveston. I must now wait for his answer.

How things are currently in Texas I have so far not learned from the newspapers (if it is quite peaceful). It is just as hot there as in New Orleans, the place where Ferdinand lives being just as southerly a location. It is extremely warm here, also, so that one has to dress as lightly as possible. Taking the summer suit has not helped out overall. The green cotton shirts and trousers are so mildewed that it is impossible to wear them; the other summer shirts are too tight; the white trousers are dirty. Washing costs much money here and must be done often. Because of this, I had to buy two (somewhat darker, quite thinner) trousers at 1-1/2 dollars and two light shirts for three dollars, by no means too much. My remaining special expenses since then are: 1) 32-1/2 C for a double barrel shotgun, which was recommended by

---

1   It is difficult to determine if he used the "C" in his original letter or the typist who made the typewritten copy of the German read it that way. Inasmuch as he speaks in dollars in some instances and then uses a "C" for dollars in others, or, it might be he is reverting back to foreign currency in his thinking.

Heye as reliable goods; 2) 2 C for powder box and powder horn; 3) 4 C for two woolen covers; 4) 2 C for an English pocket dictionary; 5) 3 dollars for drink money on the waiters and the seamen on the sailing ships (none of the cabin passengers paid more than 75 C on passage money; which Heye wanted to give me 5 C more, as the captain explained, every employed broker attaches); 5) 1 dollar miscellaneous (tip) money for my belongings from the ship in New Orleans; 6) ½ dollar for a so-called mosquito ball (necessary at night) for repelling the troublesome gnats, which swarmed in masses on my arrival in New Orleans (they are not here yet); 7) 1-1/2 dollars for a small blue silk neck scarf.

Before every further unnecessary expense, aside from these transactions, I suffered no loss or important loss, other than all footwear on the sea where the dominant damp air results in mold. I have hung out the goods mainly in the room and scattered tobacco around to guard against moths. I also take accurate consideration of the money against thieves of which rascals of all species overflow here.

That is, dear Mother, unfortunately is all, what I in my so limited situation have to write to you. The solitary time which I, in a manner of speaking, must spend here will be very long. I will write you further from Cat Spring at the same time hopefully with Ferdinand. I want particularly to discuss the circumstances with him and the costs combined if not incorrect that have brought me here. So when I reach Ferdinand, perhaps he can arrange to make the necessary provisions on the unexpected.

So then I close with a hearty farewell on you and Cal.
Your hitherto unlucky son,
Louis Engelking

Strange handwriting
Ps. Schlüsselburg July 11, 1844

New Orleans April 20, 1844

Dearest Mother!
The little good news which you hear from me at this time, I dearly want to send in advance. I am well myself, and about seven weeks ago left my dear wife and son well at home. I undertook this trip to the United States to search for my brother, Louis; I found his grave yesterday in Carrollton[1] 10 miles from here; he died October 8 last year of yellow fever. I will, of course, relate to you in order the things that have happened since my last letter on June 7, 1843, which you hopefully received through Hollien and have reviewed.
On June 9, last year, my wife, after a hard labor, successfully delivered a large youngster. I had sent a courier to the doctor about the delivery, but it occurred before he arrived; we have the little one named Carl Siegismund. On June 20, I returned back to my house with my wife, whom as you know, awaited her confinement at her relatives. Now I hoped my life would be happy, when suddenly on July 15, my wife became ill with high fever; shortly thereafter my small son, and towards the end of the month, me, the caretaker, so that nothing remained but to let Robert Kleberg transport me and my family to the best nursing. There all three of us, one after the other, were very sick, and different doctors had to be called very often.
On August 21, I received two letters from Louis, of which the contents are enclosed. They described his great

1 A section of the City of New Orleans.

irritation with the inconvenience of departure, and in lieu of going to Texas from New Orleans, he went to St. Louis. Louis believed, that because St. Louis lies more northerly, it would be cooler than in Texas; it is to the contrary much hotter there in the summer. I did what I could do under these circumstances, and I wrote Louis the same on the following day and told him that the letter exchange was so uncertain, that it was not feasible to agree on a specific day to meet him in Galveston or New Orleans. He must await the discontinuation of yellow fever in New Orleans and then come here. Since then, I never again received news from Louis.

On October 1, I was in a condition with wife and child to return back home, the poor young one nearly died of hunger over and over; my wife's milk was almost gone again and again, and there was no cow milk to drink at the moment. He was in reality smaller and lighter than immediately after birth. I walked over my farm; it offered a deplorable sight (it had been entirely forsaken). Of all poultry—ducks, turkeys, chickens—I found four chickens again; a greater portion of my hogs were missing; the cattle, of course, remained but had sporadically annihilated the fencing of my garden and had completely killed and broken down my beautiful peach trees throughout. After I had managed to attend the most necessary things, I felt renewed and lucky and contented, with a hearty wife, who could not be better. Only by her side with my small son under my free roof do I feel full contentment; never feel I small boredom as I did at home. We all are revived again, my wife could give full nourishment again and my son developed so he is large for his age and is always happy and extraordinarily lively.

October and November passed, always hearing nothing

from Louis; the longer the time fled, the more of an anxious foreboding I had and became really gloomy. I sent a horse to Houston to meet him and gave custody to a man who was sick a long time and incapable of caring for him and turned him out. The yellow fever lasts until the middle of November in New Orleans. I had determined that if nothing came from Louis by the beginning of December to search for him cost what it would. Toward the middle of December, I made my preparations and hired a reliable man to remain near my wife. Of the 400 dollars which I had received in April in Houston, I had some 30 dollars remaining and sought to raise the balance of travel money from my friends. I rode to many, but no one had money until finally the merchant Sieper at Industry promised to disburse the missing 40 dollars in Galveston. He actually had no money either, but a quantity of bales of cotton and every time a steamship from Galveston traveled up the Brazos, he went with his cotton to Galveston to sell it and asked me to go with him and he would give me the missing money. We shipped out in the beginning of January and were not more than 100 English miles under way from San Felipe when the boat ran against a large tree lying in the Brazos and tore such a great hole in it that it sank in two minutes. Sieper's cotton flowed separately down the large river, and I could not leave under the circumstances, and I was obliged to return home and noticed after five days of wading more detrimental results to my health.

I tentatively had to give up the trip and began vigorously on my farm work. I planted 80 peach trees again, began to plow, fence my cattle which, irrespective of all misfortunes that followed me, ran about 90-100 head young and old, and in the beginning of March wanted to plant the first tobacco, when I had the opportunity to sell my last domesticated horse for 40 dollars. I immediately abandoned all, borrowed another 30 dollars from Sieper who during this time had returned again from Galveston and left, this time, however, to Houston by horse. Three times I had to ride through swollen rivers and arrived after great difficulty in Houston from where I left by steamship and had no difficulty. I forgot to mention above that when the steamship sank on the Brazos, I wrote to Dr. Engelmann in St. Louis to search for my brother and if necessary, place an announcement in the newspaper. Eight days before my departure, I learned from Engelmann that my brother had come eight weeks earlier and asked if he had heard from me, but momentarily he did not know where he was. I believed then my brother to be alive and well, although I was speculative about his long and mysterious stay in St. Louis and then disappearance.

I arrived in St. Louis on April 6 and made my way immediately to Dr. Engelmann and learned to my unpronounceable dismay that the former communication was mistakenly placed on order of notices in the newspapers, and that a short time earlier, a German had told him that Louis Engelking had left St. Louis in September the year before and departed for New Orleans and had died shortly thereafter of yellow fever in Carrollton. I immediately departed and arrived here four days ago and drove here with the full terrible knowledge. Louis was in the worst fury of the yellow fever when he arrived here near the end of September and set out from here to Carrollton about an opportunity to await for passage to Texas. Two days later, he became ill while staying with the guest keeper Benoit, and about seven or eight days later would become a victim. He did not lack an attendant or good medical help, according to the accounts given me by respectable persons, but he almost never wanted to take the prescribed medicine. He received a respectable burial in a church cemetery in Carrollton with a fence around it and an upright standing stone on which is written.

> Here rests Ferdinand Louis Engelking born at Schlüsselburg (Germany) died at Carrollton of yellow fever October 8, 1843. Peace be with him.

His estate will be administered under judicial supervision. By opening his bags, 95 dollars in cash was found, and the other things consigned to an auctioneer for which 194 dollars was paid. After disbursements, there was a 16-dollar balance left, but you may hear of another charge of 45 dollars by the courts for keeping custody of the articles until the sale. The foregoing 16 dollars and the silver repeater watch which Louis had received from our deceased father were handed to me by the curator and the things removed. Where the remaining money is remains a puzzle. The packages for Sacks and articles without worth and not for sale were also turned over to me.

It is impossible for anyone who comes here from Germany during the time of yellow fever which rages in New Orleans from August until the end of October to be here and should regulate his departure as to when he arrives here. Now Louis had the unfortunate idea that he must go to St. Louis. Presumably had he been a bit longer in St. Louis, he would not have rushed to his death. The unrest and fear which I saw in his letters increased daily, and have overwhelmed me with painful feelings since the news of his death, which I cannot forget. The anticipated arrival of my brother had so pleased my wife, and when I come home alone, I cannot speak of the disappointment.

A bundle of letters was also delivered for me here. It contained a letter from you, one from Baumann, one from Auguste, one from Schieffer and Amalien, one from Bauer and finally one for Mr. Robert Kleberg. I found no message from Louis.

Many thanks for all the love you show to me. I do not know if I have time to write all my brothers and sisters in that I will depart early tomorrow by steamship for Galveston and will travel directly from there to Houston; the last 60 miles from Houston home I must do on foot. I will send this letter on a Bremer ship in Galveston where I should have a couple of hours, so I need to proceed. I cannot write anymore now.

Galveston, April 23, 1844

As I stopped my letter to you in New Orleans, a cold fever manifested itself and twice I had a strong chill. Yesterday, I arrived here, immediately took medicine, and luckily by yesterday evening stopped it. Not wanting to walk home from Houston under these circumstances, I tried, although I did not want to do it, asked to get credit from the merchant Kaufmann of Bremen against an allotment on your credit. He says, of course, he momentarily has no money, but he offered me a very good horse and whatever supplies I needed out of his storehouse. I joyfully accepted the offer, and after selecting what I needed, charged to you a sum of 118 C Lsdor[1]. After it is delivered. Kaufmann will go to Germany this summer and return in the fall. You may send the entire sum to me by the time of his return or better direct it to his main business, C.L. Brewer and Son in Bremen to his attention, E. Kaufmann, to dispatch to me.
I have so much to write yet, I cannot put it all in order. If only I were safely home and found wife and child well as I left them. Then I want to write again within the next four weeks or more. I have written and given to Kaufmann separate letters on the exchange with you. Now take care and greet all brothers and sisters to whom I will certainly next write.
Your true son,
Ferdinand Engelking

---

1   Obviously, some currency known in Bremen.

Strange handwriting
Ps. Schlüsselburg June 6, 1845

Pecan Grove June 9, 1844

Dear Mother,
My letter from New Orleans and Galveston was mailed from Galveston and departed by Bremer ship immediately and you perhaps already have received it. Mental agitation and physical stress caused a fever which reoccurred twice and brought me down. I took a large credit with Kaufmann in Galveston that he sent you that showed an exchange of 188 Bremer Talern, a good horse with a saddle and bridle, a 145-pound sack of coffee, 33 pounds of white sugar, 2 gallons of cognac, and 13 dollars of base totaling locally 90 dollars and 86 cents. The good horse happily carried me home, the river having fallen a degree earlier, unexpectedly spread out by more rain, and I had to ride around almost 100 miles. I arrived home on May 2, found my wife and child well, and we have remained so. It was too late to plant tobacco. I lost none of my livestock during my absence. Although a hard year followed me, which you learned from my letter, I have regained my valor, have more soul contentment than ever, and am confident everything will soon go well, if God will protect my wife and child. I wish to owe no one and to do nothing to anyone and to be certain that they owe me nothing.
                                                August 30, 1844
I was interrupted when writing, and various things have held me up ever since it became cooler. I, wife and child have been spared considerable illness during this generally unhealthy year. My son and I had a few light attacks of the usually hot fever, and my wife, as a

consequence of an attack of fever, had to take mercurous chloride[1] and got in trouble in June through careless drinking of Cremor Tartori[2] with considerable severe salivation, which healed after three weeks. Now, we are all well, and the sickly time of year at last in the interior of the land is mostly gone; whereas, in the seaport of Galveston, the yellow fever momentarily rages and will not end until October.

One can appropriately classify the fever here in four classes:1) the so-called cold fever[3], which lasts at different lengths (1, 2, or also 3 days); 2) quite finished and then reoccurring fever[4], (intermittent bilious fever); 3) the hot, never quite recurring but at times reduced to yellow[5]; (remittent bilious fever) and finally, 4) the yellow fever[6]. The first two species which occur in the area require only limited treatment by nature and only require necessary medicines to their quick cure without doctors. I am always so careful to have the necessary medical supplies at home and, therefore, save many rides

1 Mercury Chloride.
2 He probably means Cream of Tartar, a potassium hydrogen tartrate, or potassium bitartrate, a fine white powder, which is a byproduct of the wine-making process; a crystal precipitate that forms during grape fermentation. It is often used when beating egg whites to increase heat tolerance and volume; it is also used to prevent crystallization of sugar syrups.
3 The common cold.
4 Probably hepatitis, mild to moderate to acute.
5 ditto
6 Yellow fever is spread by mosquitoes that breed in and contaminate water, a discovery made in yellow-fever infested New Orleans when someone, without thinking, covered his drinking water tank one year preceding Yellow Fever Season. His was the only household in the neighborhood that didn't develop Yellow Fever that year; whereas all of his neighbors had it.

Pecan Grove June 9, 1844

to the doctor. (Medicines here are, of course, only available from doctors; there is no pharmacy). Pharmacies are very expensive, and the neighbor must go six or eight miles in an emergency to fetch necessary medicine which one who is naturally down and ill cannot during that time. I do not want to provoke such carelessness as others do.

The third type of fever, remittent bilious fever, is also by good attitude and nursing and the early assistance of a good doctor seldom dangerous; bloodletting right at the beginning and strong waste and laxative together with good diet help most. The yellow fever is only found in the seaports and the near surroundings. Both of these last classes of fever are particularly threatening to new immigrants from Europe and those who come in the summer. Ignorance and carelessness, poverty and greed, excess and malnutrition through inappropriate nourishment, I believe, on average bring about most of the deaths of those who arrive during the hot time. Philipp Sack[1] died on June 5 of high gall fever[2]; the doctor was called too late for him to recover. The newly inconsolable widow has within two months of his death, neglected all feelings for outward appearance and begun a romantic adventure, so that her stay with the Roeder family crumbled over it. Whether she will soon marry again is yet to be seen.

1   Philipp Heinrich Ferdinand Sack, Higher Regional Court Junior Barrister on probation, married 6 Sept. 1840, Sankt Johannis Evangelisch, Vlotho, Westfalen, Adolphine Auguste Theodore Ploeger, his first cousin, according to Church Records in the Family History Center of the Church of Jesus Christ of Latter Day Saints. (According to the film under her name, it was 4 Sept. 1840, Evangelisch, Schlangen, Lippe.)
2   It was probably acute hepatitis.

A brother of the above, Ferdinand Sack, was also one of the unlucky victims of the senselessness of coming here in summer. He was attacked by fever towards the end of June while walking from Houston to San Felipe, arrived at San Felipe and died two days later.

Four children died this summer in Cat Spring, one of Robert Kleberg's, one of Lewis Kleberg's, and two children of the four-year-deceased Louis von Roeder. The grief in the family is great. Auguste Ploeger arrived here this past winter, lived for a while with Sacks until she, because she could not put up with her sister, Theodore, went to my in-laws. On August 14, she married a German named Sarrazin[1] who immigrated here from Paderborn ten years ago. He is a strong, industrious man, who in the ten years that he's been here, through his handy work, has acquired so much that he will do well and will be good to this person.

January 15, 1845

I have let this letter lay a long time in hope of getting a letter from you. Finally, Hollien came back from Germany on the first Christmas Day. He brought me a letter from you and sister Auguste but over a year old. Hollien retains that he departed earlier from Bremen with this letter (written by you in October the year before), but I believe he pretended that these events are the latest news I received from you, and it pleased me that you are still so well as I can tell from the familiar writing. I, along with my wife and already 19-month-old son, am well and contented. If I could only see you once again

---

1 One of the founders of the Fayette County settlement called Ross Prairie, the Sarrazins' descendants were successful merchants in Fayette, Falls, and Williamson Counties. They were the ancestors of U.S. Stage and Screen Actor, Rip Torn.

and introduce you to wife and child; this hope I do not give up and already plan in the spring of 1846 or 1847 to come and spend the summer with you, providing I can put together the necessary significant funds. The plan can, to be sure, come to nothing, but it is, of course, a hope for success.

I have hired two capable workers the whole year and give each eight good cows and calves, in addition to free board, laundry, tobacco, and necessary clothing. I have plowed and enclosed a very nice field of 11 or 12 acres this fall and winter and think I will make in this year a good harvest on corn and tobacco. Both of my workers will prepare the field and build the necessary tobacco sheds, pending I pay them the cattle and perform the necessary domestic transactions. I want to bring tobacco from this and next year to Galveston, if it goes well, of about 10,000-12,000 pounds, which I will bring to Bremen and sell. One such method would not exactly ruin a trip.

You said in your letter you would like to see my life here. It is really difficult to give you an idea in a few words because a rural lifestyle here is so extraordinarily different from that of a German. You buy meal from the miller, bread from the baker, meat from the butcher, etc.; all these helpers are non-existent here. I grind my own mais-corn (Indian corn) on my own hand mill, as a general rule early in the morning, exactly enough for the whole day, occasionally more, often only enough for a good appetite, which we all three always have. My wife sifts the meal and stirs it with cold water to a mash, usually only enough for a meal, the bread tastes much better warm than cold. The mash is put in an iron pot, the pot placed on glowing coals, a tight-locking lid placed on it, and glowing coals placed thereon to cover it 10-12 minutes, and the bread is done. It has a brown, hearty crust around it that is brittle, and when broken, is white inside. Americans almost prefer it to wheat bread (rye bread is almost unknown here). I, on the other hand, would prefer wheat or rye bread if I could get good kind. Children eat it extraordinarily hungrily, and I do not doubt that it is the healthiest bread in the world.

Now I want to give you a concept of the meat custom. There is here only the notion of beef and pork; sheep are a rarity. A family of four is estimated to need an average of 1000 pounds of pork or 250 pounds each a year. Each farmer who has lived long enough in the area raises enough hogs to hold back some for breeding, his single need for supplies, and perhaps a substantial amount to sell. An exception to this is the large slaveholder, who seldom can raise his need and thus must buy from the small farmer. Fattening them (on the average is around one year), the butchering begins one at a time in the winter when it is tolerably cold (this is not often and only by north wind; at the moment for example, I am wearing summer pants and bare shirt around here; one takes all bone out of the ham and shoulders and hangs up the bacon, shoulders sides, and hams in the smokehouse after they have lain a day in salt. The bones are eaten fresh and seldom spoil.

Oxen are slaughtered the entire year. Beef is increased extraordinarily until the prices sank. A grown steer of 600-800 pounds is worth 5-8 dollars. If beef is necessary, one drives the steer out of the pasture into the pen, shoots him, lets the blood run, loosens the hide, opens him, takes the entrails out near the head and neck, which are thrown away for the dogs and pigs. The remainder is cut into quarters with an ax, transported to the smokehouse, and at times, depending on the warmth of the year, cut into larger or smaller pieces, salted, and hung up to smoke. I tend to pickle one-half of the meat because when it hangs a long time while it is the hot time of year, it will be unpalatable. As soon as the beef gets low or becomes unpalatable, another ox is slaughtered. When many neighbors reside near each other, they agree upon a sequence in which to slaughter and always have fresh meat. I only have one neighbor in this agreement and would waste much meat. As a rule, I slaughter every four or five weeks, a small calf; I've not yet raised a large one, inasmuch as I have not yet had my first cow three years.

The hide is dried and sections sold, particularly the thin pieces. The sale price of the hide is from 6-8 cents (2-1/2-3 pfennig) per pound. The tallow is extracted and part cooked into soap and part made into candles, which burn up hastily in our drafty houses.

I am enlightened by the enclosure from Schieffer. It gives me great pleasure that my good friend shows so much interest in me. I have studied through his attachment; it is very clear that his speculation for you is very primary and feasible and apparently of greater benefit. But here in the country where I live, the arrangement, costs, supplies, and work are too expensive. Should you see Mr. Schieffer, thank him in my name for his gracious information, and tell him I send greetings to him and his lovely wife.

         Galveston, March 24, 1845

I let my letter lay around again as the idea occurred to me to have you come visit me over here. Three weeks ago Kaufmann sent to me your dear letter of October of the previous year, next to the bundle of shirts and socks. I was so pleased with all of that and I need not express to you how grateful I am. I am here momentarily to collect the money and in a hurry to get home again. It is planting time there. After receiving your letter, I resolved to move my visit to you to early 1847, and then spend a summer with you with wife and child. I think I can bring enough tobacco over to cover the trip costs; how delighted my wife already is about this you can scarcely think.

The money which you sent to me through Kaufmann I want to use for the most part to purchase a young Negro woman or employ a man to remove the harder work from my wife.

I have two neighbors, both of worthy character. I live only a distance from one (he resides two English miles or nearly an hour away from me); the other is not friends as we all live sociably. I cannot lock my house if I leave from it, and I push a post before the door. No strange passerby will go in such a house, as long as I have been in Texas, yet if something could be stolen outside. Once a Negro stole a hatchet, after which I turned him out in terrible weather, had compassion, and offered him food and drink.

The widow Sack[1] after scandalizing people by living months with my brother-in-law, Otto von Roeder, has married him the beginning of this year.

The dowry money for my wife I could not raise; my father-in-law wrote to the King's Counsel Zieserock in Glogau that the dispersion is lost; the circumstances are so that I have only a remote expectation to recover a small portion of the money.

The crate which you sent to me through Baumgarten has

---

1 See note 1 page 65. Theodore (Dora) Sack bore three children with Philipp Sack. She bore five more with her cousin, Otto. Her oldest child with Sack was the only one to survive to adulthood. All five of those with Otto grew to maturity.

Pecan Grove June 9, 1844

never been received. I prepared a letter to Baumgarten on this matter and received no answer. Today, I encountered him personally and asked him; he maintains he forwarded it on to Dankwerth in Houston to my attention. Dankwerth, who also did not have the best reputation, died a long time ago; there is, therefore, nothing more to do. The barrel for Sack in which Sister Auguste packed something for me has likewise not come here.

I, wife, and child are well and happy. I have a large field to plow this year; the time until now has been favorable, and I hope for a profitable harvest. The times in Texas begin to be on the whole better, every step faster or slower forward, and I propose not be behind.

Greetings and remember me to all my dear siblings.

Love, your true son,

Ferdinand Engelking

New Orleans January 15, 1849

Beloved Mother!
Today, it is already four weeks since I, wife, and children left to come to see you. I had made plans early enough to arrive for your 75th birthday. But here in New Orleans there is a shortage of ship passage opportunities, and we have been stopped for three weeks. The ship, which I finally found, will sail from here in four or five days. Because of the ice in the Weser, I really wanted not to go to Bremen, and for this reason have booked passage to Antwerp on the Belgian ship, LOUIS. If the ship makes a very fast trip, it might after all be possible to be in Schlüsselburg by March 4. My intent was to return home before the hot time of year, a plan which now must be modified. Your letter and those of my dear siblings I received just before I left through Constant[1], and their delightful contents gave me great pleasure.
Should this letter reach you long enough before my own arrival, please let my brothers-in-law and sisters tentatively know that I soon will make a trip there and back. My decision for this trip has been subjected to many hindrances, and although it has been so many years since I have seen you, and I so wanted to see you again I can assure you, but this trip has caused many doubts as to whether my responsibility to my wife and children would allow it.

1 Louis Constant, a visionary idealist became a charter member of the Cat Spring Agricultural Society in 1856. One of his ideas was to make Constant Creek, named for him, a navigable stream connecting with the Gulf of Mexico and thus creating Millheim as a port. His impractical ideas and outspokenness got him in trouble with the Society, and he eventually returned to Germany.

A year ago, however, the obvious sorrow of my wife[2] resigned me with the determination to make the trip. If wind and waves are favorable, please expect us in the beginning of the month of March.
Your true son,
Ferdinand Engelking

---

2 Obviously referring to the death of her father at Cat Spring on November 30, 1847, at age 71.

Bremerhaven

On Board the FRANZISKA October 3, 1849

Dear Brother Schieffer and dear Amalie!
Yesterday I arrived after a stay in Bremen for four days. All went without mishap until we got there, and you would be amazed to hear that we have passage with 46 cabin passengers. There are about 16 more...and about 100 deck passengers.
The indignation among the cabin passengers over the ship's booking agents and how they were deceived is great. I have found accommodations quite good and seek to be acquainted with a better gathering of passengers. I have found them really distinguished. So far, aside from Dieks[1], I list: 1) Professor Klepp of Minden (not my earlier teacher, but the younger brother, about 40 years old) with family, 10 persons, among which one is a grown daughter; 2) von Stein from Cologne with wife and daughter; 3) Titus Mareck, delegate of the farthest (political) left, from Steiermark in Austria with wife and child; 4) a family von Rosenberg from Memel or Königsberg[2], 13 persons, including three young married

1 Unidentified elsewhere.
2 Peter Carl Johann and his second wife, born Amanda Fallier, von Rosenberg, grown children from first wife, deceased, and younger children from second wife. Memel, now Klaipeda, the capital city of Lithuania, is near the much larger city of Königsberg, now called Kaliningrad, and located in Russian territory. Peter Carl bought part of the Nassau Plantation near Round Top from Otto von Roeder, who took over the property from the indebted Adelsverein. The von Rosenberg family became prominent in Fayette County, especially in Round Top and La Grange.

or engaged couples; 5) head master Dr. Hertzberg from Minden, fugitive by reason of threatened arrest as a Democrat or high informer in addition to a number of very good outstanding young people of all types. The amount of tasty delicacies and refreshments which are all over the cabin here and in the passages is almost inconceivable. The cost to the ship after the breakfast ends this morning will be very high.

We took advantage of the abundance of things during our stay in Bremen, buying partly necessities and partly useful things; I have a crate of about 100 pounds packed.

In the Weser Turn 8
October 8, 1849

I have not closed the letter yet because of six stormy days delaying our departure. This morning about 6 o'clock during a strong wind the anchor was raised, and now we feel the first waves of the sea. The pilot will take back this letter with him.

Our passengers have bit by bit adjusted to their narrow quarters and are good sports. I have found here an acquaintance from Texas, named Wagner, who came for a young wife. The Holzapfels (sons of the deceased I.C. Holzapfel in Paderborn) are also here in steerage, four hearty young people; Victor Bracht's[1] bride is also in steerage; in general, is the entire group as chosen, all

---

1 Businessman born in Düsseldorf, he was sent to Texas in 1845 to represent German colonists' interests. In 1848, he wrote a history of Texas entitled, Texas im Jahre 1848, which was not translated into English until 1931 by Charles Frank Schmidt. According to The New Hand Book of Texas, Bracht's bride was Sebilla Shaefer, whom he married in Indianola in 1848. That date must be a misprint or he was married twice, the first wife having died shortly upon arriving.

Democrats "of the first water"[2]; many farewell letters will be written to the friends in prisons; and many perceive with the lightened breast the coast behind disappear, which until the last moment view threatened danger. The best to me up until now is the family von Rosenberg, and it would please me very much if they, as they already wish, could settle in my neighborhood.
At this moment, the seasickness has begun, the first symptoms show around me, and on that, I want to close. Thank you for all the love which have shown to me; if you come to visit me in Texas, I hope to show you a small amount of what little I know. Greet Reuters, Carl with his wife, Baumann, and Julien, and stay well.

Your sincere loving brother,
Ferdinand Engelking

Editor's note: *The early series of letters from Ferdinand Engelking to his family end at this point. According to notes compiled by a descendant, Rudolph Engelking of Sealy, who traveled to Schlüsselburg to study the church records and uncover other information there, Engelking's father filed a will on August 9, 1848, and died September 15, 1850; however, earlier we learned that the father was deceased. Engelking wrote a letter addressed to the mother early in 1849; however in this last letter, Engelking addresses his letter to his brother-in-law. According to a family history published by a descendant of Engelking's sister, Malwine Reuter, the father's life span was 1759-1830 and the mother, 1775-1848. This would seem to indicate that the mother filed the will on August 9 and died the latter part of 1848 after filing the will, but the news had not reached Ferdinand before his departure. In his letter to his brother-in-law, he does not mention his mother's death.*

2 A figurative expression for pure ideals.

Editor's note: *Mathias Franz Schieffer, Ferdinand Engelking's brother-in-law, husband of Engelking's sister, Amalie, was the author of the following letter-diary. The beginning is missing. It appears to have begun in October 1850 at which time he was in England awaiting something, probably his wife's arrival, so that they could go on to Texas. It appears he left Germany in a hurry, and she had to settle their affairs.*

***

Consuls set out in motion, and as similar processions do in Germany, many curiosities showed. Therefore, it was strange to see if here and there a large clumsy Englishman attempted to walk on his big feet on which they all suffer so considerably.

October 30

I even discovered from the American Consul how to watch circumstances regarding the ships and have determined to wait to surmise if it would appear to you most acceptable to wait in Bremen.

November 1

I believe that there are many here who sanguinely (what I interpret as "ravenous hunger") hope with all their might that the revolution in Europe ends.

You would not believe how deadly tiresome and yet costly every day here is, as one has nothing to do but loaf. The vicinity, especially the Isle of Wight, is lovely, but the weather for outings is too raw, and the cost for the necessary guide for a single person is too high in price.

I cannot stop the bad habit of occasionally thinking about Hinsberg; today for example, it is a workday here, whereas during the day there it is seldom when the magistrate's office is not closed. Here, one day is like the other; in the early morning it is very cold, and I remain awake in bed until almost 8 o'clock, smoking tobacco,

On Board the FRANZISKA October 3, 1849

drinking coffee, and finally about 5 p.m., having a late lunch, and just as nothing occurred the entire day, nothing at all occurs after the meal.

Today I received your dear letter of the 29th of last month. I thank you for your love and affection and remain as up to now yours in love and truth.

November 3

I froze last night and I do not think pleasantly about frost and the Weser[1] together. On the latter above linger all of my thoughts and imagination.

November 5 to 10

> You land of ale, you land of port,
> You land of ladies, you land of lords,
> Were I out from you once finally forward
> You are as cold as your people,
> (Which I felt yesterday, I feel today).
> To me but beats the heart so warm,
> I dream, I had in my arm
> my angelic far off love
> Who remains constantly good and true to me.

I will hear German spoken to me here again, and the cold chains me to the chimney in the rented room. For your trip today you have the finest weather. May that continue.

> A man with gray hair
> Of fully fifty years
> I sit there in my room
> Alone with my misery.
> One has often sworn to me,
> "Ach, had it also a mouth,
> It would no doubt have
> made my sorrow known."
> So, Sir, I will not refuse,
> You let your billows carry
> My dearest calm over here

---

1 A river running through Germany which empties into the North Sea where the current day Port of Bremerhaven is located. The city of Bremen further south used to be the seaport on this last leg of the Weser, and this is from where most ships embarked.

Had turned ears!   to me.

Galveston, December 22, 1851

Dear Father and Dear Brother!
From farther away, I wish you a Merry Christmas and with the New Year, all luck, well being, and prosperity and inform you at the same time that we happily arrived here on the 19th of the month. You already know about our arrival in New York from the letters of my dear wife and are anxious to receive some more news about our journey, and willingly communicate with pleasure the things I have seen with my eyes.
Without having done anything wrong, I had to silently leave behind the homeland like a felon and my life, friends, and relatives to spend over six weeks in England, when my dear wife followed me thereto on November 11, and on the 14th, we left behind South Hampton, and at St. Albon's, Europe, on the steamship, WASHINGTON, which as you know, brought us to the New World on the 28th of the month. This trip was, however, more difficult and dangerous than you would or anyone would have wished us. A journey so far at our age for people who until recently were used to comforts and orderliness was a terrible exertion, to which one would not want to subject oneself, even for the fastest and highest priced means of transport. Think about the complete lack of movement on the waste system, the entire change in cooking, this latter reason causing the inevitable interruption of natural discharges, and added to that, the swelling of the sea. I did indeed not have as strong men have true seasickness, although I have not always remained free of headache and dizziness; my poor wife was ill directly from Bremen as were some people with whom we became acquainted and remained

so the entire journey.
We experienced the first storm on November 21, but on November 26, we had the worst and most dangerous, whereby captain and crew took the most extreme efforts to contain it and from which one could hope for nothing more from human help. In such storms, glasses, plates, chairs, passengers, and everything else are tossed all through the ship, as you might perhaps imagine. For example, on the night of the 21st, a high swell crashed 15 feet overboard and covered the paddle boxes, which would unfailingly have washed away a helmsman if he had not clasped the iron rails with his powerful arms and legs, that in places caused flesh to be shed from his back. On the 26th, we were awakened from sleep early by the violent rocking of the ship, and as I came on the deck, the sea was already considerably high, though it did not prevent me from going to the upper deck on the side of the steering helm towards the smoking and bar room in my usual manner to puff my morning cigar. To me, this was fairly simple to do; then as I was doing this, I saw the captain on the other side of the steering helm pull out of the closet a chronometer, sextant, and ships' papers and hasten below deck from where I had come out, which possibly could be closed if a swell spilled overboard, and I now in the safety of the smoking room decided to leave but had hardly treaded out on the open deck and was caught by such a powerful swell, that I grabbed fast with both arms onto the compass cabin, a potentially fatal situation from which the first steering man saved me. The storm wind now began to roar and under its rush, the large beautiful ship to moan and creak as if it wanted to tear itself out of its seams. The crew (135 strong men total) bravely manned their posts, but the storm became so strong that by continuing on its

course, the ship might be broken, so a last attempt to escape was made, and finally, with unspeakable exertion the ship was turned and steered south of its course to the relief of the passengers. How necessary that latter was, how much mental suffering and discomfort the poor passengers felt shows what indescribable fear prevails, as on the afternoon of the second Sunday of our journey, the engine died suddenly, and no one but God had any idea how long we would be drifting around in the open sea without drinking water, in that the engine prepared seawater. After a horrifying hour of fully frightened waiting people, the damage to the engine was determined and the pallid countenances lost again.

The small beds in our sleeping cubicle were over each other[1] and shortly before all this happened, one of the upper bed stands broke, so I, as the heavier, lay in the lower and my wife in the bed-stand over me. In the stormy night, my wife took my bed, so that she would not fall out, and I lay in the upper bed between the bed stand and the luggage and fastened myself in this position and watched through the long night like this during which each time the ship threshed around, I always stiffened, as one does in a carriage on a rough road, developed a bad pain in the curve of my back. Some passengers, who for reasons did not fasten themselves to a position, were seriously wounded, and today there are many who show black and blue bruises. Otherwise, I must confess that I am very lucky, if one can feel that way after experiencing this from early morning until evening of the 26th.

One cannot give an accurate description of a more terrible, more beautiful, and more splendid sight, so to speak, as the depths of welled up ocean and

1 Upper and lower berths like on a train.

magnificence of the sea storm which I saw as I was fastened between the main mast and the area of the cabins, filled with trust in God's wise and gracious providence, that the idea of danger dwindled; now as one sails along high above them and looking far out, one does not think of 50 or more foot rings of green and white bordered circulating wave pileups as they are concealed by their shine. On November 27, the ocean was calmer, in the evenings, it was smooth as a mirror, the pilot came out on board, happiness reigned throughout the entire ship, and the next morning nearing nine o'clock, we lay in New York Harbor.

Much praise of the city's beauty and surroundings is made; we have not seen much of it because of much heavy rain at the time of our arrival, and there was nothing much there to please us on the other two days of our stay. We had two choices of how to continue our journey - continue by sea or go by railroad to Lake Eire, then by ship to Cleveland, then by rail again to Cincinnati, and from there, by steamer on the Ohio and Mississippi Rivers down to New Orleans, and we decided on the latter.

At 4:00 p.m., on December 1, we left New York at which time a fierce dry cold wind was blowing from the streets, and an alarm sounded seven times, whereby burglary, robbery, and murder had been committed. Soon after we left, it got dark, and as we hurried through the region that could be seen at night, we noted the difference between German and American railroads. The trains in this place consist of five passenger carriages (with no difference in classes or prices), each holding about 50 persons, each is heated, and has a water closet provided. The carriages have front and back doors through which runs an empty corridor with upholstered seats on each side for two persons, so that, for example, one gets in the first carriage and can go through all of the carriages. Up to that point all is good, but traveling in this carriage all night with no support for the back and head, and the wheels bumping over poorly banked tracks, that when rushing fast, the carriages thrust about and one has to hold on as one did in a coach on the old German post roads. And worst of all, is that every Tom, Dick, and Harry, including the educated class of Americans with some exceptions, chews tobacco, and consequently incessantly spits.

In any case, we arrived here in Dunkirk on Lake Eire near noon on December 2 somewhat disheveled. It appeared so peaceful and quiet there that one could not look at the water and realize that it had cost so many lives and it was so rough this time of year on the days before our arrival, that no one would venture to navigate it, so we were awakened on December 3, and three hours later, the anchor was raised. We were accompanied by two men who had lived in Cincinnati many years, Hammer, a Catholic priest at St. Mary's Church, and Murmann, a lawyer, whom we had met on the sea voyage and for whose good advice many were indebted. We climbed out of the ship in the dark of night over a couple on shore and experienced more terrible cold from the hill behind which lay Cleveland. At the first inn to which we came, we had breakfast and saw Lake Erie at its worst than we had earlier in a calmer state, and going on 10 a.m., we left on the train again and arrived in Cincinnati December 3 at 11:00 p.m., so that in an unbelievably short time, 934 English miles between New York and Cincinnati lay behind us.

The railroad from Cleveland to Cincinnati has been completed recently and goes for long distances through virgin forests in which here and there is a clearing where a settlement is built and one can see where thick snow offers a picture of loveliness and solitude, which caused me to notice a couple of seats ahead of me two people whom I would not expect to be confined to this land, one asked the other "Wo mögge de Lück wu lewwe?" Note: (The foregoing is dialect from the Rhineland meaning "Where would the people live well?" I attempted to pursue my discovery further had both men not gotten out at the next station and had I not had to push through many people and dreading the verbal admonitions.

Prospect Hill
February 25, 1852

It will appear strange to you that after fully two months of being gone, my first letter comes from the New World, and I must confess that I am upset with myself that I received your dear letter of last December 15 fourteen days ago. Hear my excuse. I did not write any more in Galveston; we had many lovely days there, mild as they are in Germany the beginning of October, and after the trying journey, we had to make use of movement in the free air and restoration of health, and did not have lights by which to write. I also believed that you would surmise that circumstances would prevent me from writing so long and that you would be reassured about us from the letter my dear wife wrote from New York of our safe arrival in America. I eventually became significantly ill in Galveston, and the doctor there advised us to leave the city as soon as possible and to hasten to the healthy country; we hurriedly notified our brother-in-law of our arrival and requested of him, especially for my suffering wife, if we might convalesce from our wearisome journey at his house, where we finally, Heaven be thanked, have continued to our complete recovery.

Galveston, December 22, 1851

To pick up again the subject of my earlier writing, on the evening of December 4, we left Cincinnati by steamboat again, a city of more than 100,000 residents, which up to now, was the smallest we had seen in America, and arrived ten days later in New Orleans (where we stayed in the finest and most expensive hotel of the world, the St. Louis) and then left early on the 17th again by steamboat. The first night on the Gulf of Mexico was very stormy, and the entire group was with small exception seasick to a high degree in five minutes. I belonged to the exception, but was so miserable that although I could stand on my legs, at 3:00 a.m., I got out of bed because I was soaked wet from water coming through the locked window from the rapid succession of swells through the night.

I am afraid, of course, that if I want to speak in such detail of my journey again today that I will not end this, but I want to say that I prefer to relinquish travel in America, be it by water or by land; we overcame our hardships and forgot our discomforts fast, and will have a long time to think of them.

How do we like it here? This question is easier asked than replied to; of course, we hope that it will please us better than it has up to now. Texas is more a land of acquisitions than pleasures, and he who does not want a life of hunting and riding will be deceived by the reclusive life one must find. Of course, no where in the world is a place where people can go without torment. I suggest the distressful reaction over the rowdy simpleton sheep in Heinsberg[1] that has driven me out of my homeland.

April 1852

---

1 A city on the Wurm River near the Dutch border in the present-day state of North Rhine-Westphalia.

We have finally received all of our possessions of which the extra articles from the delivery to Mr. Heinmann and the questionable worthless paper here will probably eradicate their value in a short time. The additional papers my wife forwarded to you, dear Brother, may now well be a torment to you, although one cannot know what evil, persecution or intrigue or stupidity might hatch. I feel sorry for you, although it gives me satisfaction that you had a satisfactory second attendance in Heinsberg, as the people there now understand how disgusting life was to me there. It is untrue that I promised to take Heinrich Legros with me; I merely said to him when he expressed his apprehension that he would become unemployed by my outspokenness, that I regretted the situation his wife causes making it impossible for him to emigrate and that he is able bodied and could find his escape. But it is true that he has cried out to me for years to help him. And it is true that I have always counted on his help, whether or not he agreed with my viewpoint that he should emigrate. With no evidence, he questioned my help or service and thinks his shoemaker or tailor or whoever only renders to him the courtesy of giving him credit.

I hardly know anything of Texas except what I have seen from the journey here, and from that, it is too immensely difficult to outline a true picture of the native life, especially when I have not ventured to understand the diversity of tastes of the people. You can occasionally mention to Mr. Thönneshen what seems to you to be required from my letters, such as that my wife and I are healthy and she sends greetings. I would write to Mr. Thönneshen myself, if I knew what to say to him, but I wish so much that he could find a place there, for I strongly doubt that he would like it here, but if he cannot find work there and he wants to come here, I will gladly

Galveston, December 22, 1851

help him use his strengths and skills. All cash he raised or raises for me you can receive from him and acknowledge, for it is certain I have no means to accommodate it, and if you find nothing hindering you from using it privately, please make use of it. If for any reason, you cannot do this, then pay Mr. Thönneshen 500 thaler. My wife agrees that out of the interest earned up to now from the 500 thaler from dear Father, make small gifts at New Years and on his birthday and from what remains, buy yourself ham and sausage or a glass of wine for you remain in our affection and thoughts. The 500 thaler you might use in case of an emergency or in the event of something exceptional or necessary or desirable whichever, for your brotherly love. Also refund yourself for all expenditures you have had on your trips to Heinsberg and Cologne for me, and what is raised on the auction of my articles, take as a gift as proof of my appreciation for your management.

I have so often wanted to end this letter and sent it off, and then would, as now, become so wistful that I can go no further. God grant you health, perhaps decrees that all of us will see each other on this earth again, and shields you and us. Take care.

Your loving son and brother,
M.F. Schieffer
P.S.
Prospect Hill, April 22, 1852
    My address is
    Austin County
    Swearingen's Post Office
Never forget when writing: "per steamer via Liverpool" otherwise letters go via sailing ships and take a very long time.
My wife heartily greets you, and I still think that when

you greet Mr. Thönneshen that you indicate that it is not quite so easy for self-maintenance and not to rejoice so much to my enemies there, or better yet, communicate to him that there isn't any difference. It am so heavy of heart that I am convinced I will not send this letter. Of course, I will not stop and you will finally have news of us, and be it not so favorable as you wished. Again, we send our heartiest greetings.

Austin County, Texas
Swearingen's P.O.

May 10, 1852

To Ludwig Buchholz Esq.
Georgetown
near Washington City
District of Columbia
I have just now received your communication of March 24 of this year and hasten with the answer if you are still there. It makes me very sad, and seems a bit strange that you feel so uncomfortable in a land of freedom that misses not only all pleasantries, but also goes without the comfortable German family life. Would it comfort you to know that you have a fellow sufferer here, who often silently curses the tattered reaction in Heinsberg; because life in the German homeland has suffered, I have tried methods brought here with me, hoping to produce, but have not yet succeeded and have strong doubt that in my years to be able to operate a farm, although I have 60 acres, the property of my brother-in-law (by which I pay remunerative costs and have a home). Of course, it would be too difficult to explain everything I want.
Today, I restrict myself to replying only to your communication that my love of German life has not made me like many things here, and that this is, in comparison to other states of the union, which are much more favorable. I can not yet pass judgment and would gladly give you my brother-in-law's point of view which would require that I delay my answer until the next postal pickup. All I know is that there is considerable cheap land here, the price of cattle is steady, and German immigration is very strong throughout the United States.

As to Indians, robbers, and thieves, I have heard nothing in the inhabited parts of Texas, and our journey here was quite peaceful; for example, during our trip, our carriage with our belongings was blown over by a norther and hail storm on the open prairie and left unguarded two days while we were two hours away at the next house. Finally, your question as to whether a family with only a little money could get by. I am too unfamiliar with the native population to reply, but I feel I can say that he who can work gladly works, and through toil and deprivation of the first years and is not frightened back by not having significant funds will eventually find advancement.

On your last question, I will always gladly find information. Of course, I hope for you that you will have found small pleasure in your temporary stay. Greet your wife, daughter Valesca, and the other children from my wife and me, and I remain in high respect

Your loyal
M.F. Schieffer

Editor's Note: *The following paragraph was inserted but not written to Buchholz*

May 12, 1852
I was tormented in my youth; therefore, I have been here four months and am not dead but buried alive. Who can know if and when imprisonment comes to an end! Is the need of pursuit in the old world a disease rather than having equality; here idleness is only tediousness to the community.

Finances

My brother-in-law Ferdinand exchanged for me:

1. An exchange on Oct. 4, 1850, over		397.62
2. Two exchanges on Oct. 21, 1850	899.05	
	900.00	1799.05
3. Paid to Ferdinand for bill from Vornkahl		19.50
4. Exchanges on Mar. 26, 1851, over		
a)	1200.00	
b)	1300.00	
c)	1338.30	
d)	1400.00	5238.30
5. Three exchanges on June 18, 1852 over		
a)	1200.00	
b)	1226.95	
c)	1250.00	3676.95
6. Six exchanges on Sept. 12, 1857 over		
a)	1242.06	
b)	1300.00	
c)	1500.00	
d)	1600.00	
e)	1700.00	
f)	1800.00	9142.06

Cologne September 11, 1853

Dear Ferdinand,
Today is exactly three months since we said "goodbye" to each other in New Orleans, and I am summoned out of my apathy and seriously reminded to send you news from us. The series of long illnesses I have suffered has slowed not only my body, but my mind, and I have postponed the strain of writing up to now.
Beginning with a sultry and ending with a sensitively cool voyage causing the usual discomforts, and those with unclean and bad food, traveling daily, and two Frenchwomen who formed an alliance, we finally landed on July 27 at 2:00 p.m. in Havre[1]. We remained there four days because Customs gave us so much difficulty, and we finally gave up our plans to travel further by train. We embarked again for Rotterdam by steamer for 32 hours in very stormy weather, from which Amalie became ill. From there, we could have sailed the Rhine upstream for 24 hours; however, our luggage hindered us again to make use of the fast ship and we ended up at Düsseldorf and took the train on August 4, arriving here at 9:00 p.m. at the Rhine Inn, where we have remained for four weeks, partly because it is inexpensive, has good food after the long deprivation, and especially because we could not find lodgings suited to us earlier. We rented lodgings here six days ago in a house, No 7 Klein Sandkaul, and as soon as permits, we will arrange the visit of our relatives from Paderborn and Schlüsselburg from whom we already have had letters since our arrival. Our dwelling has an outer cellar with spacious storeroom, well, and rainwater pumps in the cemented

1   French port.

floor, and above these behind six large windows facing the street, a living and visiting room, joined by our bedroom next to a cubicle for wardrobe and next to the yard, a kitchen and two spacious rooms near the fence corner.

I can tell you nothing of what I brought is worth in exchange. First, I tried to collect that on the middle of the calendar month and received nothing from a protest of default, so I relinquish the hope to collect anything from moneys in their possession. Europe is experiencing partial and not quite productive crops in succession causing grain-money lenders to speculate losses.

How are your wife and children, Klebergs[1], and how does Albrecht[2] receive his bath?

We heartily greet all, also Maetzes[3] and Wennocks[4] and Mr. Nolte[5] and hope that you have already written to us. Take care.

Your brother,
M.F. Schieffer

---

1. Ernst and Louise von Roeder Kleberg, Ferdinand Engelking's wife's oldest sister and her husband.
2. A child of Louis (decd) and Louise von Roeder Kleberg, he died while a child.
3. A political refugee from Germany, he came to Millheim and distinguished himself as an educator, being hired by Ferdinand Engelking to serve the community as a school teacher.
4. Apparently Engelkings' neighbors but don't show up on 1850 census.
5. Frank Nolte was a shoemaker in the community.

Cologne September 11, 1853

In September 1853 while unpacking the articles I brought back from America, I found these pages which I wrote with pencil during my illness in Texas during five long weeks of salivation when I was unable to speak.

***

December 14, 1852
Have Charlotte cook only thin soup or I cannot eat. Just as in September ten years ago when I suffered gastric-rheumatic fever, three and one-half months ago I got diarrhea on the third day here in Texas, where I have had the severest illness since this past September with abdominal inflammation and the disgusting salivation replacing the diarrhea. During this time, I repeatedly stood before the entrance of eternity, and now my famished, ailing body in a state of farthest exhaustion and depletion will recover with God's help and the constant attention of my dear Amalie.
    I cannot drink wine
    I endure much have done
       well on a starvation diet.
I do not know, I seldom eat of course, each time little, and of course am not too energetic. How long have I been silenced, when will I be able to speak again, if only I could go on my crutches.
At night I always hang my head over the bed in front of a chair back. Today my lips are very swollen against my tongue, make it thinner and the sips smaller.
My memory has suffered so that the little I remember is in no chronological order. These holes make distorted facts. I tried to yawn and met with such pain because I could not open my mouth. I was so feeble and swooning.
For Christmas I wanted to give *Coopers Romance* to the Klebergs; my sporting gun, my pistols, and saber to Ferdinand; and Walter Scott's *Romance* to Lina. But I

could only relinquish my sick chair to the Christmas celebration.

***

On another page, I found written in pencil what I remembered.

***

On Tuesday, March 15, 1853, we left brother-in-law Ferdinand's home and arrived at San Felipe at 3:00 p.m. I grasped little of the fact that, as I feared, Amalie had inconvenienced herself to turn our entire carriage into a bed for me. As we arrived in San Felipe, we sat with our heads together driving through the 20 far-scattered houses, joined a half hour later by my brother-in-law who shot snipe, to await the steamship on the Brazos for a further journey, but having reached a temporary end. After four days of eating bacon and eggs varied by eggs and bacon, we decided to abandon the idea and transfer our belongings overland to Houston and arrived there by carriage on the last Monday. This city, just 14 years old, makes its name through beauty and liveliness of its streets and through the splendor of commerce, lying on Buffalo Bayou, where one can travel from there by steamer to Galveston, approximately 80 miles away, in 9 or 10 hours, where I could resound a full "hallelujah" early in the morning.

Often what we first lament as misfortune, we later recognize as a gracious arrangement of providence, which saves us from tragedy. For example, I lamented we could not leave Millheim earlier because I was still too weak, so had we departed three days earlier, we would not have been delayed by the shipwreck which the steamer ARTHUR suffered March 19 in the Gulf of Mexico. And had I not suffered a dietetic weakness that delayed us a couple of days longer in Houston, we would

have found our end on the Wednesday before Easter when the steamer FARMER blew up in Buffalo Bay.
On June 7, 1853, at 4:00 p.m., we departed on the steamer MEXICO from Galveston 72 days later, the last 14 of which were already so intolerably hot that it hardly cooled off at night. The greatest heat was usually at 11:00 a.m., and it had already reached 90oF, driven by the lack of wind over the hot sand, causing sweat from all pores. Our night quarters were incomparably bad and unforgettably hard and were under a surrounding netting shield against mosquitoes, constricting ones breathing. Goodbye Galveston! I hope never to see you again and as promised, turn my back to you with happiness.
On January 9, 11:00 p.m. (Galveston time), we reached, after a very peaceful but slow trip, this place on the Gulf where it takes on the waters of the Mississippi. The border of both waters is from north to south as far as the eyes reach, about a six to eight foot wide border of spray and sharp driftwood. West from the border is the Gulf water, still greenish-clear, easterly from there that of the Mississippi, against which the ebb and flow to resist is strong enough and is yellow and dirty. From this place one sees in a northeasterly direction first the lighthouse and soon land, and in approximately an hour, we were in the mouth of the great stream.
On the morning of July 11, going on 10:00, we finally arrived in New Orleans and departed from there the following evening, going on 9:00 with the American three-masted GLOBE, Captain Baker. This ship has too much draught (draft) about it from a steamer that towed it out to sea, so we are at holiday this Sunday on the wide stream and tortured by countless mosquitoes. We lay at anchor in the face of Belize, one of the saddest regions of the world of 500 residents, where 350 are alligators.

On September 19, 1853, a small package arrived at the post office and the work woman will be sent home with it. In Texas I would without hesitation carry a small package home myself, as I often personally hauled home from the store sugar, wine, beer, and coffee. In Galveston each morning around 5:00 a.m., the men appeared with handled baskets on their arms and made and carried home their purchases for the day themselves. On the whole, one gives away one's position in America, if one does much for himself. For example, one personally polishes his own boots or he cares not whether or not he goes along with dirty boots and shoes.

Help is not always available and is very expensive, for slaves must be bought by reason of the universal aversion of the American to entering a contract or hiring someone. The served whites feel offended if one offers him a tip; only the blacks accept one, or if need be, a "green" (that means an immigrant) if he is in a free contract relationship. In the inn in New York, I put my boots before the door of my room and did not find them there the next morning. Upon inquiry, the house servant appeared with my blackened boots under his left art and gave them to me for a half schilling to his outstretched right hand, and delivered much more to me each time.

Schieffer's Residency Application

Transcription of my petition to the police at Cologne, purpose of my settlement:

***

Dear Royal Police:
To your honor I obediently register my petition to dismiss that two years ago as notary in Heinsberg with my wife, Amalie Louise, born Engelking, presented ourselves here two months ago to make this my permanent residence. My yearly income is not large, approximately 800 thaler, and I have no children. I have a suitable residence here at Kl. Sandkaul No. 7, and it is my intent to remain in Cologne, so I ask
"The Royal Police: I want to register my name in the local registry in an inexpensive residence."
Cologne
October 11, 1853
M.F. Schieffer

***

(Editor's Note: This apparently was a gift to his wife's sister and brother-in-law.)

Cologne October 19, 1853

Cologne
October 19, 1853
Dear Baumann,
>That Amalie after long desire
>First yesterday again found the cake
>which recently tasted so good to you,
>Will shortly herewith to you discover,
>If now in the flavor combine
>With you all your love,
>So do to us to know manifest;
>And are we then, as now, health,
>So send we yet more,
>It pleases us so much.

***

(***Editor's Note:*** *To literally translate dissolves the rhyme. The late Dr. Gilbert Jordan, Professor of German at Southern Methodist University in Dallas, published a book of German verse entitled GERMAN TEXANA in which he put into rhyme in English many familiar German poems that he had translated. Here is Flora's amateur effort of the above.)*

>Amalie, after much looking round,
>Yesterday finally the cake found
>Which tasted so good to you,
>And shortly will send it on to
>The one whose best taste is united
>With all his dear love and is requited.
>So thankful are we to know
>That your pleasure can follow
>When we yet more will send,
>And our love will see no end.

***

Or non-poetically speaking: "Let your enclosed honeycake taste good and reach you safely."

***

Remembrance:

On the steamship, we sailed the Ohio and Mississippi from Cincinnati to New Orleans. In the ladies' parlor, we met two families from New Orleans whose company we found not too bad. One of the ladies was born Creole, and her entire family live purely as French, and she is so graceful, and she and her family only speak French, she told us as she rocked there in an indispensable rocking chair. To have service is to them inborn in their race, and she described with biting scorn the English-American whose free ways provided ill humor against traditions and customs. As I remember the three daily meal times, the American fashion is all conversation ceased and all ate and left. If the Captain invited us to his table, we forgot the laughter of our Creoles, took our places after which followed the loud bells for the remaining company. Then came the many clumsy and left-handed, many in stoical quiet, and awaited their places, speaking among themselves, either working the jawbone or in soundless silence, devouring their food so fast that even Christ would not have finished his table prayer before he would gaze at the empty dishes. Those very silent fast meals no longer surprised us as a rule, for at the American inn in New York where we stayed, we had already experienced those who ate, stood up, and left the table before late comers had seen the menu and ordered. About two days before our arrival in New Orleans, we landed at Brennholz in the neighborhood of a sugar plantation, where someone brought some cane aboard ship, which were sliced in pieces somewhat thicker than

Cologne October 19, 1853

our asparagus and peeled and chewed out the juice after which we threw the fibers away. This sweet crop provides the luxury of sugar thanks to the work and sweat of blacks.

Cologne February 7, 1854

Dear Ferdinand,
We learn from Julien[1] (according to your letter of December last year) that you are without news from us and surmised that our circumstances with regard to the exchange were good. My letter of last September 11 is probably lost, although I brought it to the mail myself. I enclose a copy of my first letter with this one and will not prepay it.
I cannot inform you of much news from us, only of small matters. In Reuter's[2] opinion, none of the Schlüsselburg inheritance comes to you, for you have been advanced money three times in the past, which he has arranged himself. Reuter has looked over the matter and written Baumann[3] that what remains each of us should receive 200 Thaler in the near future, paid in a lump sum, to especially the three sisters[4].
My dear Amalie and I are very well, thank God, and are both as healthy and fat as we once were. We live very modestly, have energy, eat heartily, and go easy on the pleasures.
From Julien's letter, we also learned that last June you had another son, and we are happy over that; and, of course, if you have more children, hope that it the other gender.
From my wife and me hearty greetings to you, your wife,

1   One of Engelking's sisters.
2   Engelking's brother-in-law and husband of his youngest sister.
3   Another of Engelking's brother-in-laws.
4   There were four sisters, Amalie Schieffer, Auguste Baumann, Julie Bernau, and Malvine Reuter.

and children, Klebergs, and all neighbors and our loving thoughts. Take Care.
Your loving brother,
M.F. Schieffer

Cologne June 6, 1854

Dear Ferdinand,
We received today with such great happiness your letter of April this year that I cannot recover and will answer this day without delay. We are so pleased to finally learn (tomorrow it will be a year that we left Galveston) that you and children, including the unacquainted to us Ludwig, are healthy, and we hope that the wish for his always earth-appetite will be lost. We and as far as we know from Höxter (there is from Schlüsselburg and Paderborn no direct lively correspondence) as well as the relatives in Westphalia are well.

I scarcely expected to hear that you have sold Amalie's bridle and saddle for such a good price. The accumulated interest of your debt on us up to April 1 of $320 can be cancelled and I calculate none for the next year as the sale compensates you for the trouble and expenditures for us which you have had since our departure. In the coming year, I will then calculate 10.4 percent for interest and the remaining .6 take off which I believe I told you earlier.

The news and change in the neighborhood is of much interest to us; we ask you to give Klebergs, Valeska (now Madame Langhammer[1]) and Nolte congratulations, and greetings to Maetzes from us. How pleasing it must be to you that the school has begun there and that Maetze will head it, and that there are still some educated families in the neighborhood, and in general, so many support it and that the store has brought about this favorable thing.

---

1 The Klebergs' only daughter, Valeska, married Gustav Langhammer.

Where have Wennmahrs[1] moved and where will
Langhammer-Klebergs live? What would come out of
the schoolmaster (Joke - brother-in-law)?
Have you nearly completed the store building at the slope
of your hill on the east, so that out of the windows of our
former bedroom or from the north porch entry one can
see the entry? And have you expanded your acreage? We
hope the current harvest may be, with God's blessing
over it, compensate some from the previous year. Have
you received no rent from Christian[2]?
We are passably well. Bernau[3] is pensioned; we do not
know how much he has. None of his children is with
him, and he does not worry himself about them. Julien
has great ability; Arnold[4] has made the teacher
examination and George[5] is in the last semester at
Göttingen from where he will probably come to
Paderborn next August. Amalie Bernau[6] is at Reuters.
Baumann is to receive the Order of the Eagle third class;
they invited us to visit, but that will not occur for the
reason that in this year, we are avoiding all unnecessary
expenditures.
Let us not let our letters lie. As soon as a letter comes
from Galveston or perhaps from there, or after news of
you comes, I will write again and for now will close with
the wish that all goes well for you. You have said nothing
of Albrecht Kleberg, so we hope that he is well. I think
with terror about the heat which will rule when this letter

1   This must be the same family to whom he referred earlier
    but spelled Wennocks. Nothing shows up on early records
    of people with either spelling being in the area.
2   Probably an immigrant boarder.
3   Another of Engelking's brother-in-laws.
4   The Bernau children, niece and nephews of Engelking.
5   ditto
6   ditto

Cologne June 6, 1854

arrives. There was not so much sickness there as in my peak year.
My wife and I send our best greetings to you, the children, and all friends and acquaintances.
Your loving brother,
M.F. Schieffer

Cologne June 23, 1854

To Viedebandt[1]
Dear Friend,
We are both well, and our life goes forward in the familiar ordinary fashion, and the impact of repeated visits to the summer theaters in Mülheim[2], of course, offers too little to report. But now I have something new to apprise you of, so I will not ramble. Yesterday at 6:00 p.m., we went as usual, if the weather allows, to the Scheinbridge[3], and we were not yet halfway, and we saw coming towards us Pochhammer[4] and wife, now married three weeks after a honeymoon in Switzerland and Italy and stopped at Klein Sandkaul for them to catch up. We accompanied the couple to the cathedral and separated from them there, as they wanted to leave for Bonn about 9:00 p.m. They had postponed the trip until earlier today, and we sat and chattered for hours from yesterday evening until dawn in our loiving room.
He is very pleased that you have improved yourself, even though it was painful for him not able to see you, and he asked me to greet you and the family from the Straten[5]. He would be stronger, his wife is not exactly attractive, although a very friendly appearance. He is head toll inspector in Pomerania[6] in a region two times smaller

1 Unknown; never mentioned before.
2 A summer theater on the Ruhr. This is also the German spelling for the settlement of Millheim in Austin County where the Engelkings lived.
3 Possibly an upscale area in the heart of the city near the great cathedral, the latter for which Cologne is known.
4 Obviously someone both Schieffer and Engelking knew.
5 This appears to be a German or Danish surname.
6 Once a province of Prussia, it is today a region in northern

145

than Washeberg, whose two-syllable name I have already forgotten and felt himself very lucky.
My wife and I greet you, your wife, and the sisters-in-law. Take Care
M.F.S.

Poland.

Cologne July 6, 1854

Dear Baumann,
I would ask that you please excuse my long silence to your last dear letters and kind invitation to visit you this summer, that I would so happily would like to accept. However, I must ask that the offer to visit you be postponed until the coming fall. Although, thank God, we are very well and also strong; of course, my dear wife struggles with a combined disturbance and general uneasiness with the heat and likes to stay home. But also we speak our mind on something more and that is we cannot spare the money to make a trip now. I have tried as a good provider to make our pound annuity last and find it hardly sufficient for the annual expenses of the household budget. This will now hopefully be more favorable in the future, particularly from the 6th of last month.

Ferdinand sent pleasing news dated April 21 that we have received. He writes that he and his are well, in their neighborhood a couple of families have settled down, his store will soon be ready, he has 20 acres planted with a good harvest likely, and will go to Galveston in about 14 days and send us some money from the sale of furniture left behind and taxes. Then he says:

"I ask you not to be nervous if I am not prompt to fill my obligations as I would like. I can assure you that my annual circumstances are better, and I can gradually payoff the due payment."

Coming back to my earlier subject, if the heat ends and money will be in the bank, we will be happy again to see you, but for now in my opinion, the trip must be relinquished.

How is your father? Hopefully, you are all well. We have had other news at all times; Arnold always wants to write, and he is also well and will soon be out of the military service.

My wife and I greet you and Auguste, Julie, Anna, and Arnold,
and I remain
Your loving brother

Cologne August 4, 1854

Dear Ferdinand,
In case the original unexpectedly failed to reach you again, enclosed herewith is a copy of my last letter to you which I wrote almost two months ago. This duplicate I believed I could send earlier in answer to your communication which you said in your April 21 letter would come from Galveston. I know now it was your intention to travel to Galveston in approximately 14 days and things like that intention are not so punctually carried out in Texas as one here believes. Anyway, is it possible, if not probable, that you really did not go as you have written, and you had not received my letter of a year ago, and that you pretended ignorance. Up to now, I have received no further correspondence other than that of April 21 and a letter containing the money of the sale that you calculated is lost.

From earlier communicated reports and news, I know that we all are well in spite of an entirely rainy summer and have had heat, the previous month at noon 26 or 27-1/2 Grad, whereby workers died of sunstroke while harvesting, and a steamship from here to America, the lovely FRANKLIN, had a most particularly unlucky star to rule it, which joins the HUMBOLT and CITY OF GLASGOW, the third in less than a year.

I don't know much to say, although I am interested, of course, in your communication of circumstances. Is your enclosure of the house ready and how is the garden enclosure? Have you also prepared a bar in the store, and are Quenzel, Brosig, and Hollien regular guests yet? Also my old friend Schneider[1]?

1   All neighbors of Ferdinand Engelking.

Hearty greetings to you with wife and children and acquaintances from my wife and me, and take care.
Your loving brother,
M.F.S.

Cologne August 17, 1854

Dear George,
Enclosed is the acknowledgment of your dear correspondence of day before yesterday enclosing the money due out of the Schlüsselburg inheritance.
Now that we have money we have determined to visit our dear relatives of the responsible father of so long ago, and to express to you also our best thanks for your poem for our silver anniversary. We will leave on the coming Monday morning at 11:00 from here and will be in your midst in the evening.
Should that, however, not suit Uncle or Aunt Baumann, write us and we will come a week later.
We hope to find you are all well and lively in a couple of days and will delight in the presence of each other.
Your dear Uncle

Cologne October 7, 1854

Dear George,
Your long awaited letter arrived here today and, along with the report that you are healthy and passed the exams with brilliance, has made us very happy. For this reason, we send you 22 Thaler towards the obliteration of your schooling in Göttingen. Whether and what we can do for you depends most importantly on the long awaited and not yet received American telegram. Of course, we prefer to do our bit towards your future strengths.
I always have such very cold hands and feet despite good fires, that I can scarcely hold the pen and ask that my wife take on the correspondence and greet you heartily.
Your loving Uncle,
Dear George,
Your uncle called me out of the kitchen to take over his correspondence because he could not write anymore with his cold hands, and I am very pleased to do it if I knew what to write. I feel sorry for you poor youngsters; I wish we could contribute more to improve your situation. If only the exchange 3000 finally came, which is still held by a merchant in Texas, we would be so happy, for it would make a distinct difference in our income.
I have written your mother in the past week, and she has invited us to visit this fall. We had promised Aunt Baumann to come thereto earlier in the spring, but now the Circus Renz[1] causes so much to discuss that I have uninvited us, but to date we have heard nothing and we must wait until the early year.

1 Circus Renz was a German circus company. It was established in 1842 in Berlin by Ernst Jakob Renz (1815-1892) as Circus Olympic and existed until 1897.

To know that Amalie is always a little anemic makes us very unhappy; it will make us very happy if she wants to visit us early in the year; the question is whether she will like it here as much as in Höxter where she has Emilien as a playmate, and if you return, you as a playmate.
Now, dear George, let us know now and then how you are and take care.
Your loving Aunt
Amalie

Cologne November 26, 1854

Dear Arnold,
I have read the first printed production of your PSYCHE. Under your name, you are introduced to the world as someone with whom readers are unacquainted and whose future has promise. Had you not sent the booklet to me, I would not have enjoyed this; although not too old, I am, of course too temperate. Yet I am willing to read the lovely old myths it relates, and also the wedding night, page 29, which might not please everyone if misread, and to me that expression "in the stranger," the beginning of something happy is a misrepresentation of the entire small fragment. What appears to me to be more thoughtful, although not every reader would agree, are the many things that brighten the place where the old Grecian ruler wants to be.
Please receive my best wishes that you shared with me the charming road you traveled in your dreamworld and have shown me the treasure of your rich soul.
George has written to me again (before May 23) and informed "I have now finally decided to stay at my father's home as long as I enjoy respectable treatment, as I want to separate "..."preliminry setback I hope next year to be free from the military"..."Mother is uncertain of the time of travel"..."Received from Ernst a letter of September 28, 1854, in which he says he's well."
How are you getting along with your father? We are comfortably complacent here, one day after another. A couple of times we were at the Circus Renz and also at the theater; however, only to hear the great singers or, as they are called, music princes, Roger and Formes. But now only average singers and plays perform, and because

the unfortunate weather does not let us out of the house, we have done nothing as to the arts in the month of November, and for that reason, all is somewhat backward.

Take care now, dear Arnold. Your aunt says "hello" to you as well as Uncle and Aunt Baumann and Anna.

Your loving uncle

Cologne June 8, 1855

Dear Ferdinand,
Finally, the so long awaited news arrived from you this morning, namely your dear correspondence of April 2 this year, for which I thank you. I will exchange to cash as soon as possible. Unfortunate that you believed that you could not write without being able to send money, and I have remained uneasy for almost a year.
I am very displeased that Mr. Longscope gave you so much trouble. Of course, please be assured that I am very grateful to you. Earlier you believed Longscope quite able to pay. Should he still be in a decline, would you please attempt to get him to agree on three payments, if he still momentarily has difficulty. I cannot judge what would be best, and I am sure you will look after my best interests.
My wife and I and your remaining relatives are well, being closer to inform you. We are confined here by much unhalting expense; I barely taste wine anymore; we drink beer and will be thick and fat from it. I have very little to tell as it is not as easy as you think, although the exchange is easy.
I thank you for the news you have communicated, and also deplore how unpleasant it is. Have you a new Nolte or do you manage the lovely new store yourself? It appears to be a good way to go if one did not have the colossal borrowing in that there is a strong growth to the population (have you gotten a girl child?) or expected? The fact that Dr. Nagel[1] settled down in your

1 Dr. Herman Nagel settled in the neighborhood and became a leading citizen. However, at the outbreak of the Civil War, he refused to take the oath to the Confederacy and fled with

neighborhood is of great value to all Millheim. You will scarcely believe how much this news interested me. I forgot to send the enclosed printout in my last letter, and it will now be obsolete.

Your letter has been en route a long time. Another handwriting over the address was "via New York Bremen."

Have you learned anything new in Galveston? Is the merchant Baum well again; what became of his brother's debt to the water doctor and how is he, Muhr, Wolff, and Bishels?

Hopefully, you have found your mare with her yearling. But when Säccolet is not available, which horse do you ride and how do you plow between the corn rows? Have you still the wild ones, Goodeye and Stängo, or what are the speedy animals named?

It has been more than two years since we left Millheim, and we often think of it, and it pleases us to learn that your children make progress in school We believe that if Fritz[1] is somewhat slower than Sigismund, he will still be able to find his way, and does not particularly in Texas need to be exactly a scholar so long as he remains healthy. The youngsters have grown a great deal; we always think of how Carl[2] came to our chamber in the morning with the words, "gu'n Morgen, ja so muss man

---

his oldest son, Charles, via Mexico, to Missouri. Charles Nagel was the same age and close friend of Engelking's oldest son, Sigismund. After the war, Sigismund traveled north to visit his old friend and through Nagel met his wife. Nagel went on to building a career which eventually led him to be appointed Secretary of the Interior under President William Howard Taft.

1 Engelking's second son.
2 Charles, Engelking's third son

ja sagen, wenn man'n Stück Kuchen haben will.[3]" The nimble Carl really enjoys going to school.

Greet all friends and acquaintances from us and a hearty greeting from Amalien to you and from us both to your wife and children. I remain
Your loving brother,
M.F.S.

---

3 "Good morning, so of course one has to say if one wants to have a piece of cake."

Cologne September 19, 1855

Dear Ferdinand,
Arnold and Amalie Bernau were here at the same time to visit and I was so busy that I am so late and just noticed your letter of June 24 this year which I received four weeks ago.
Arnold has also read your last letter and of the Wilms swindle enjoyed at our expense. We hope that the entire Wilms claim will not always be lost to you, a substantial loss, and that such a casualty would spoil your entire merchant position. On the whole, I see you still have your large cattle herd and the duplication of farming which can back you up; have you a new Nolte, or your crown prince betrayer, to help the merchantly construction?
As to the Longscope trickled agreement, I can attest my best thanks and through time the claim will be cancelled; on things like that one must always calculate on scarcity or else even an honorable commonplace fellow.
My brother is now to become land dean, another position he transfers, and his income bettered. Amalie has cut the enclosed article out of the newspaper. It caught her interest as did all of us that find news of Texas relevant, that immigration is increasing and railroads progressing. Amalie wants to write to Fritz, so I must clear the desk and do this with sincere wishes that you with wife and children are well and these lines might touch all friends and acquaintances and extend my heartfelt greetings.
Take care,
Your loving brother
M.F.S.
Editors Note: *This ends the correspondence in this*

collection between the German branches and American branch until the following which is a span of 15 years.

Ha Drs Extension H & T.C.R.P

Bremond June 18, 1870

Dear Uncle Schieffer,
Do you still remember little Sigismund, the oldest of your Texas nephews? I am he, now a grown man, one inch taller than Father. I am no longer in Millheim, but last winter on a visit home read Aunt Reuter's letter to Father in which she communicated in detail to us how all the relatives in Germany are.

We should have written to you long ago. Why Father is so bad about it, I do not know, and for me, the beginning was too difficult. I must simply explain so you can understand how things have been with us in the 15 years since your departure; in the entirety bad.

Our family has significantly increased; besides the grown sons, there are living still four brothers and four sisters from 16 to 1-1/2 years old. Our oldest sister, Ida, died a year ago of epilepsy; she was already 12 years old. The 16-year-old Ludwig will soon reach manhood; he is very sickly, and all other siblings are healthy; they are in order: Albrecht 14, Lula 11, Marie 9, Lina 7, Valeska 5, Wilhelm 4, Ferdinand 1-1/2 years old.

Those who are of the right age have to attend Maetze's school 1-1/2 miles from our farm; at your time, Mr. Maetze was already a teacher in Millheim; you do still remember him? My oldest brother, Fritz, is 24 years old, and Carl 22; both already strong men, somewhat smaller than Father;

the first has the nickname, "the Temper" because he drives a hard fist and takes no nonsense from anyone, and the latter is called "the Dancemaster" because he prefers to play and dance rather than do hard work, although he can work better than either of us if he only wants to.

For 18 months I have worked as a clerk on the railroad; I do well finally; I earn $75 a month and have already saved $1000. Fritz has been here for six months also, foreman over workers, makes $45 monthly, room and board naturally free. Carl drives cargo 100 miles from here with a personal wagon; he makes good. Only the elders do not do as well as one would wish, although Father has significantly enlarged his field, and so, of course, stays on the farm, although Father is not practical.   Our store is as good as gone; because of the war[1], we lost four slaves, much money, cattle, etc. After the war, the cotton weevils always destroyed the harvest, and it appears that Father just will not get back on track again. In the aftermath of the war, all value in Texas fell very much; our cattle, for example, worth $7 earlier now scarcely worth $2.50 and property in general is in exact proportion.

Mother is still very vigorous and economical and knows that her diligence and her prudence will prevent the gradual degeneration of houses. Father would also be still vigorous if he did not get pneumonia so often in the winter which is dangerous if he even suffers from a cold and is not very busy and lighthearted. Father is quite gray; Mother has changed little. Father lost the right forefinger accidentally in our mowing machine; other than the newspapers and his long pipe, Piner's LEXICON is his main pastime. Father is farming again this year full strength; unfortunately, Ludwig is too weak to help him, and Albrecht is still very young, therefore, Father and the hired blacks, whose wage is high and performance modest, must do the work, and if the crop

---

1   U.S. Civil War (1861-1865).

remains bad or theweevils come, he must do the seeding again.

Father strongly supported the revolution of the Southern States and has, because of his voting record, lost his right to office of which he will soon be pardoned. Fritz and I took part in the great struggle. I was in Virginia, where I was wounded and captured during the second invasion of Maryland, but was soon exchanged, and then Father came and nursed me six months until I was able to travel home with him, where I was on crutches a long time as the wound healed. I have to thank my father for my life; without his help I would have died.

Fritz marched with all 18-year-old sons of the country and served in Louisiana and was lucky not to be wounded. As freedom finally came, we young people were very joyful, and we gradually see how absurd it all was to bleed, but Father sticks stubbornly to the old idea. The enclosed is a picture which I send along to you and Aunt Amalie, and offer hearty greetings, and hope for a speedy answer from

Your loving nephew, S. Engelking

Bremond, Texas June 29, 1870

Dear Uncle Reuter,
Father will not have answered your dear letter of last year. He will be upset if it is too long before your letter is answered; it is too difficult for him to write; the old man has trouble with his hand. Our joy was great over the receipt of your letter; Father was especially cheered over your relation of yours and his youth, which is treasured by him.
Through a female cousin who lives in California[1], we had already learned that one of your sons is also there. Please read the enclosed to Uncle Schieffer and send it to him; I do not know his address. You can see from that, that things are not so good here as those outside of Texas might represent. Until 1861, we moved steadily forward, but from that time on, the war and its sad results reversed the earlier well being; one can soon again work ones way up if one does not immediately run into bad luck as it did with us in the last years after the fall. For example, Father attempted through all sorts of speculation to bring back all that was lost.
In the past two years we three oldest sons have stood on our own feet. Although because of my wounds I am not capable to do much physical work, I have found successful employment, and for 18 months, luck smiles on me and I have saved to be able to open a shop of my

1   This could very well have been Clara Kleberg Hillebrand, eldest child of Lina's sister, Rosa Kleberg. Clara, her husband, Heinrich Hillebrand, and young daughter fled the formation of the Confederacy, just as Dr. Nagel did (See note 1 page 157), and moved to Oakland-San Francisco, California, area where their descendants live to the present.

own and look towards a peaceful future; I am temperate and thrifty, am as fluent in English as German, but am without a wife. My brothers, Fritz and Carl, farmed cotton the first year in company but without success; cotton weevils destroyed the crop. Since then, Fritz works with me on this railroad, where he does well if only he has the necessary patience, and also earns a beginning capital. Carl drives wood from sawmills to the train which also pays well, but Carl has not showed, up to now, the discretion and perseverance which are necessary to own and manage a business. Perhaps it comes with age. On the whole, we young people could be satisfied with our situation, if only Father's circumstances might soon become better.

In the opinion of most, the conditions in the Southern States are not pleasing; in Texas is yet the best outlook, even if it has the least money, it also has small rule. Achievements of all kinds will pay well, the usual day laborer receives from 75 cents to 1.50 and board. In the mid and northern areas, the farmer earns much money; there cotton costs on the average 15 cents per pound; a man can harvest 8-10 bales at 500 pounds. And immigration has become slow. There the railroad companies erred on very strong workers by way of 250 Chinese imports which don't count. The farmer from Washington County has raised $40,000 to import German workers, and several agents from this organization have traveled away to carry out this effort. If the farmers provide what they promise, it would be a good chance for needy diligent men, but there is also much deceit here.

Only slowly is the American becoming accustomed to the large revolution in occupation on the social status of the Negro. Blacks are now born equal under the law. In

Bremond, Texas June 29, 1870

general, they make reasonable use of their freedom and are peaceable and courteous, so long as they are honestly treated. For this reason, they also like to work with German farmers because they will be paid promptly. Father cannot deal with Negroes; he is too severe, and the Negro perceives that.

I would be very pleased if one of my cousins, the Lt. for example, would open a correspondence with us, and would not forget the large water which lays between us. Brother Fritz joins me in greeting all of you dear whom we do not know; and to the aunt, your wife (I have sincerely forgotten her name) a kiss from
Your loving nephew,
S. Engelking

*The Only Photo Ever Taken of Ferdinand and Caroline
von Roeder Engelking in About 1872*
From the collection of Rudolph Engelking, Jr., deceased,
of Sealy, Texas.

Millheim, Texas January 10, 1887

Dear Malwine,
Your letter of October 25 received fifty days ago and the expressions of sisterly love therein are so moving that I found it too difficult to answer you immediately. It indeed troubles me much that our dear Reuter's health had not been satisfactory for almost a year, and what is more, what caused it, but at our age (he was more than a year older than I), we have to expect that we will not continue to enjoy good health and tolerate what ails us. That you yourself enjoy excellent health, and with your children happy, there is little more for the elders. The detailed account of the comparison of your children, and how they continue to do well, has filled me with pleasant satisfaction, and I hope that their well being might continue to grow.
From the time of my visit in Germany in 1849, I remember vividly my niece, Anna Baumann, during our stay in Paderborn, who 30 years ago was a rosy-cheeked girl of six years, a good walker who often went with us in the afternoons to coffee at Neuhaus. Arnold Bernau was in 1849 an enthusiast for the new times; he already sent contributions to the newspapers and seemed to have good construction, but also seemed to be a flyaway; it makes me sad, of course, that he has lost the affluence he acquired by marriage through real estate speculation. Amalie and Schieffer probably died with animosity against me in their hearts. From their standpoint, based on their temperament and lifestyle, I can understand it. Already prior to the time I left Germany in 1849, they on one occasion, casually led me to perceive that they would move to Texas near me. Although at that time, I did not

recognize that these casual plans had serious intent and crossed them off by stating that their lifestyle and customs at their ripe age would make them painfully aware of the shortage of comfortable conveniences here. In about 3/4 year they wrote me that they were determined to come here, that living in Germany any longer appeared intolerable. To me it would be daring. I admonished them once again to use consideration at their age and naturally assured them that if they did come, I would strive to make life for them as comfortable as the circumstances permitted.

Without further delay, Schieffer sent here a first parcel of money with the news that as soon as his money concerns were settled, he and Amalie would be coming. Schieffer knew of my position here very well, that I owned a small farm with an 18-foot square living house and a blockhouse wherein, instead of the window trapdoor, only a cattle herd occupied, whereof the expansion and the realization of my receipt formed. Also Schieffer insisted that I must promptly and to a certain degree build a substantial and spacious living house. All building materials were for such a house at that time very expensive and to hire carpenters, cabinet maker, fencer, etc. required costly special workers, and of course the greatest haste was necessary for Schieffer's arrival and would only allow the house to be partially raised. During the construction Schieffers arrived in Galveston and Schieffer became ill there with diarrhea, and the doctors there advised him to leave as soon as possible. Schieffer wrote to me and bade me to come to Galveston promptly and transport him. It was the middle of the winter in the coldest weather, railroads were not yet available, the roads were without foundation, but I, at that time yet in my strongest years, worked my way through to

Millheim, Texas January 10, 1887

Galveston and speculated on the possibility of how I could get home with Schieffer.

At that time, light steamships to San Felipe on the Brazos seldom traveled unless the water was high enough. Fortunately, I found a steamer which would take the trip to San Felipe (10 miles from Millheim) and booked Schieffers' passage on that and also brought along the unsecured luggage on board. Arriving in Columbia[1], 75 miles from here, the captain gave up going any further on account of the too shallow water. After seeking countless goods wagons for the continuation of the journey to the country, I found one and transferred us and after several days, we were on the way again. After nearly one day's trip back, we were in an isolated region and were overtaken by a terrible norther with snow and sleet, and we luckily reached and found shelter in a dilapidated and abandoned blockhouse. After a couple of days, as the stormy weather abated, we laboriously set forth on the journey and finally arrived home.

You must try to understand what impression this introduction to Texas must have made on Schieffers. Now we would jointly share the new living house as far as it was built. The next one and one-half years were the most terrible time of my life. I was justice of the peace and had arrested a person for two days for a deep insult of the jurisdiction. The man hired two attorneys and brought an action against me by reason of wrongful freedom deprivation of $1500 damages compensation and promise to the advocates a sum of the proceeds. My attorney which was expensive made such a miserable defense that had no doubt he had made an agreement with his partner that I lose and would share the spoils with the other lawyers. The jury condemned me for $200

---

1 East Columbia/West Columbia on the lower Brazos.

dollars damages compensation, so I lost including legal costs and lawyers' fees of over $300.

During the process of the actions, both of my youngest sons suffered an attack of flu; when I came home in the evening of the verdict, I found the oldest dead; the other died several hours later[1]. It was as if at that time all had conspired against me; around me was dismay and grief and great expenses and losses to be made up. The construction had also cost nearly $2000 which had been defrayed from Schieffer's money. The household would cost as much as possible to be to the satisfaction of Schieffers, things to be restored were very costly and Schieffer remained behind his expectations. Amalie gave my wife constant criticism as to how all should be done better, and in the end reduced my wife to such despair and depression, she asked me in tears if she might leave to go to her relatives in West Texas. My own troubles were always larger; the tending of my cattle herd had been abandoned a long time ago and I suffered a loss from that. I saw my ruin before my eyes if this continued for a longer time. I engaged a young man who had learned the merchant trade in Germany and began in partnership with him a trading business. It profited naturally and gave an outlook of steady improvement. At the end of the year Schieffer would become ill and came near death. Amalie and we did all possible for his care and through the efforts of sent-for doctors, he would, after a long time, regain his health. Now Schieffer decided to return to Germany. With much inconvenience, I had to once again bring them to Houston, Galveston, and New Orleans. At the last point, we were held up a long time again until I found a ship scheduled to cross over to Germany. I brought them on board and said

[1] These were Franz and Otto born after Charles/Carl.

farewell to them.

I gave them a promissory note of $3300 to reimburse them for the costs of the construction and acquisition of housewares. Upon arriving at home again, I sought to better my situation, and eliminate my liabilities bit by bit. Through diligent tending, I soon brought my cattle herd to a marked increase; my partner in the business in contradiction to the beginning, began gradually, although barely noticeable in the beginning, to drink. If I was at home, he pulled himself together, but I could not accomplish the buying of goods and take care of things at home, too, which often made my absence necessary for a long time. Then he would give good friends credit against my protests, became disorderly with the books, and held nightly drinking bouts with his friend. When I came home in 1856 from an eight-day trip to Houston and Galveston, I found him in delirious tremors; he died of an epileptic fit.

The books were in greater disorder. I was lucky to find fresh from Germany an immigrant bookkeeper to take the chaos out of the books and working independently and with each other compile new pages in the books that were orderly and set up at a glance. He was, to be sure, also an incorrigible drunk, so that I jerked a concealed glass of whiskey or brandy out of his hands numerous times and poured it away, but with surprising speed and expediency, he fulfilled his task. Over and above that, he trained for me and mine an engaged clerk (no merchant but a tanner) through instruction in the most practical methods to keep my business' books. The result was not so unfavorable as I had feared; there were things lost to be sure, but on the whole, only a small amount forfeited. Now I equipped the shop again. My clerk left much to wish for, but he was reasonable and honest, so that I did not need to be in the business myself day after day and could again tend my cattle.

Soon I began to move forward and think about paying on the old debt to Schieffers, and then in 1861, the wretched War of Secession broke out. Gold and silver disappeared out of the country; goods could only be sold for the worthless paper money of the South Confederation; good and bad debts were hastily paid with such paper money; the beef cattle for the armies would be bought for a nominal price. War taxes, contributions toward outfitting armed volunteers, etc., took great sums away. My goods-stock was soon bought out without which I had none of what I was well known for. As a good patriot, I took on the cause of the South with heart and soul. In Germany, where almost only Northern newspapers with their partisan portrayals were disproportionately read, meant that there were unfavorable opinions over the legality of its cause for the South.

As soon as the hostilities began I brought my oldest son, Sigismund, who was exactly 18 years old, provided him with all necessities such as money; he went from there to Virginia, the first war theater, and marched as a volunteer in the infantry. Here he took part during 1-1/4 years in six bloody battles without substantial numbers being wounded. Then I read in the newspaper a report over the first unlucky battle at Sharpsburg in Maryland that the regiment in which he fought was nearly annihilated; from his company only three unwounded remained, he was severely wounded and returned with the army train to the hospital and had fallen into the hands of the Yankees. Without hesitation, to save him and to free him where possible, I gathered up all gold which I still had and departed from here the next day. The connection with distant areas at that time was still very imperfect; I had to

Millheim, Texas January 10, 1887

take postal carriages or rental carriages or go some miles on foot, but beyond the Mississippi, it went better, although on long detours, and, of course, always either travel by train or steamship. In 15 days, I reached Richmond, Virginia. Prior to my arrival directly to the War Minister, I visited a citizen of Richmond at whose accommodation Sigismund sometimes stayed and with whom he had become friends. He told me that two days earlier Sigismund had arrived by ship and had been exchanged with another wounded prisoner and was accommodated in the Texas hospital. He had been rescued from the brutality of the Yankees for a truly not transportable wounded person.

As I stepped before Sigismund's bed in the hospital, he called out to me joyfully, "Good morning, Father." At my question of are you then not surprised to see me here, he only replied, "I have waited for you." The shin bone was crushed and splintered by a musket ball, and then exited again not far from the heel. Once I had lodged in the hotel and went to the hospital only during the days, I reflected afterwards that my consistent presence in the hospital might be offered and made a deal with the superintendent that I reimburse the hospital for a bed to be set up beside Sigismund's side at the usual hospital cost. Sigismund was badly wounded as determined by the masses of discharge from his injury and would cost extra for care if he was to get his strength back, so I went daily to the markets and brought back such foods as eggs, fresh oysters, young chickens, etc. Of course, it was uncertain for a long time whether or not the leg could be saved. Finally, after I had been three or four months in Richmond, a slow healing could be seen.

I inquired about Sigismund's receiving a furlough to return home. It was a long time. Finally, his general visited him himself, the furlough was granted, and now came the most difficult part of my task. During this long time, the Yankees had made great advances, burned bridges in many places, destroyed rails, and blockaded the Mississippi with steam canon boats. Getting through was difficult; a long stay in the hospital was not expedient to my health and strength which had been attacked by bad air, and if Sigismund became worse, the trip would be impossible.

After a few days of Sigismund's practicing on crutches, we, in the company of some other Texans (also some on crutches) who offered to join us on the journey left. This time I chose a route through east Tennessee. Over some small streams, the railroad bridges were destroyed, and I sometimes had to accompany Sigismund a mile or so on foot to keep him from falling and then return for the luggage and then cross the streams in leaking boats and then go ahead to find the next railroad station. I had earlier discovered that small steamers on the lower Mississippi still occasionally passed by night into the Red River, and would by our forts stop and not be noticed. After five days of anxiously waiting, a steamer came, picked us up, and happily brought us to Alexandria[1] on the Red River.

But on the way, Sigismund had developed from the wounded leg a very angry rose color to a blood red flame and spread over his entire abdomen. With the help of four men, I had to bring him into a bed in the military quarters. Fortunately, General Staabs, physician of the State of Louisiana in Alexandria, was present. I directed him to this emergency, and he was able to arrest the farther development of the illness, and in nine days, Sigismund could stand again, and the trip could again get

---

1 Louisiana.

under way.

During this time, I had my misery of yearning for wife and children, homesick to see, speak, and tend and to refresh myself with delicacies, a condition to be held back. We now took a mail carriage, which was to bring us within 24 miles of Millheim. But the vehicle was so crammed full that Sigismund could no longer endure it after the first ten miles, so we left the mail carriage at the next station. Only occasionally was there an opportunity to rent a carriage. The region was empty and abandoned. In a small area of the Angelina River, I finally found the opportunity to buy a leaky but roomy canoe. Now the other invalid with me was a great help. He was an experienced sailor and knew the streams to Beaumont where a railroad went from there to Houston. Although he had a crippled leg, he was much more robust than I. We repaired the canoe, made the necessary oars, and did so without considerable supplies which were not available on the trip. It was the end of April 1863, the weather was nice and warm, but a persistently strong south wind blew and the stream flowed forward very slowly, so we had to use all our strength to row, with Sigismund himself taking part where he could. There were a few abandoned houses on the stream which gave us no food to buy, so our small store was not satisfied. For this reason, we slept half the night on the land, and made use of the suitable moonlight to travel. So it took us three days and two nights to travel the 220 miles to Beaumont.

I gave the canoe to our fellow travelers in Beaumont and set out with Sigismund without further difficulty on the journey home, where my wife eight days early had borne a daughter. During my continued absence of one-half year, thieves had broken into my store and had robbed much.

Sigismund healed very slowly; for an entire year he lost bone splinters out of the wounded leg. In the fall of 1863, my second son, Fritz, volunteered and went to the army. He entered as a riding infantryman (sharpshooter), so I equipped him with a good horse. He served until the end of the war without being wounded and came home only once on furlough having lost his horse and to get another. Sigismund subsequently had to return as an invalid and worked in the Quartermaster Department. I myself joined the so-called Homeguard Company, guarding war captives, providing security in the interior, etc. We had no constant service.

Trainloads of re-convalescents and on-leave soldiers came through to which our house was always open for quarters and feeding for both men and horses, which kept us out of breath day after day and swallowed up our property and goods. The blockade of the southern harbors by northern ships made the necessities of life unattainably expensive; medicine was almost non-existent; a pound of coffee cost 1 Prussian dollar; the same for one yard of calico; other cloth goods in that proportion. The situation required that one heard in almost every house weaver's looms making cloth for the demand that could not be satisfied. Our opposition to the north was exhausted bit by bit and broke in the spring of 1865.

I had bought with the worthless paper money a Negro almost as worthless and had him work my field. Beyond the Confederacy, cotton brought a very high price; here in the country it brought a very scanty price, so I had collected the yields of other years and accumulated 40 bales. Many of my neighbors hid their bales in thick woods, which if Yankees attempted to confiscate, they would shoot from the sides. I had to sell my cotton for a ridiculous price; three months later, I would have obtained a price four times more. So I lost at one blow about $4,000. The Negroes (I had five of those) were declared free without my being compensated, and have since that time by their disposition and laziness prone to crime against property and security of the persons, particularly of the female sex, a large public misfortune. They imposed through their reactionary government high costs to the white population in the South, showing no favors to the race.

The now introduced bloodsucking system allows not the impoverished Southerner for a long time to rise again. Under this, for each bale of cotton brought to market one must pay $15 export tax. Once I tried to re-establish my trade business to better my position, but without success because the interruption of my presence hindered it too much during the fluctuating communications .

The impossibility of removing my old debts to Schieffer pressed at me again, and the shame over this caused me to decide that it was better not to hear from me for a long time. Since this time, I have been active through working the fields and tending my cattle and my big family. My three grown sons soon pursued their own efforts, and I, myself though, because of my age, was unable through the war years to tend my diminished and scattered cattle herd, so four years ago, I appraised the number of head to sell and kept as many milk cows for necessary milk and butter to feed those at home.

Now it is time to give you a small review of my children. We lost three sons in early childhood, the oldest daughter, Ida, a very gifted, kind girl, we lost at 13-1/2 years to epilepsy; another, Rosa, at 7-1/2 years, to dysentery. Living still are 1) the oldest son, Sigismund, born 1843, soon after the war, went to work as a bookkeeper and jack of all trades with a railroad contractor from the North to Texas, developed a good career, saved a nice sum of money, married when his contract ended in 1870 the daughter of a German in the northern states, established a farm two miles from here, gave it up because of weakness in his invalid leg, began a business in San Felipe, began well but misread the deterioration of San Felipe because of sickly location; began another business in Bellville, but because of an abdominal illness was not in charge of his shop long and became bankrupt three years later. He made a compromise with creditors of 60 percent, and in the past two years has been the teacher here. His health has since then been significantly better, but whether or not his 800 dollar salary covers expenses, he manages by his indifference to money, but his well-to-do father-in-law helps him out. He has four sons and a daughter living; three children died of illness.

2) My second son, Fritz, born 1845 married in 1871 and moved into a farm in the neighborhood of Sigismund. His wife bore him in the course of ten years seven children, three sons and four daughters, who all are healthy and, of course, alive. But for a time, madness, at first imperceptible, gradually crossing over into a regular frenzy, made him and his family poor. Then I had to take him to the county seat in Bellville, request and let a jury declare my legal guardianship of him. Then I took him to the State Hospital in Austin. Four times these attacks reoccurred, and four times he was discharged after ½ to 1 year. Fifteen months ago he returned the last time from the hospital and three months later his wife delivered a daughter; after happily having overcome the childbed, she died three weeks later after a relapse. We took the

Millheim, Texas January 10, 1887   185

seven children to our house and my wife nursed and raised the small girl with the bottle who is now healthy and strong. Fritz returned again and was discharged and has moved with the six other children to the farm; the little girl for whom we have much joy we have kept with us.

3) The third son, Carl, born 1848, has endeavored since he was 20 years old to try his luck outside in the world. But the violins which he saw hanging vanished before his eyes very soon. After somewhat over a year, he came back home after having acquired some means. I helped him get started on a farm near Fritz and Sigismund, whereof he married. He was a practical and good worker and progressed, but like Sigismund, he found farm life too troublesome; and he believed that, like Sigismund had at San Felipe, that as a merchant he could move forward faster whether or not he had the necessary knowledge. Whether or not I approved, he bought his goods and wanted me as his partner in Cat Spring, a small town five miles from here and entered an organized business, purchasing goods and cotton. Because of the distance from here and domestic and other engagements, I was not present often enough in the store, so Carl began to buy at excessive prices, wasting goods on customers he drew, and I saw after two years, that it was necessary to get out of the business and to save the larger part of my outlay of capital. Three years ago, Carl had to liquidate, and the trustee of the place paid the creditors 45 percent. In the past year, Carl has pursued a very profitable inn (tavern) in Bellville. He has six children living--five sons and a daughter, one child died.

4) and 5) Ludwig and Albrecht, born respectively 1853 and 1855, distinguish themselves neither through establishment nor through energy. Until six years ago,

they remained at home and helped tend the farm and cattle, thereby acquiring a nice sum. But from the experience of the older, the younger chooses not to follow. Against my advice chose both employment where they had no knowledge or experience; both are married. Ludwig has a daughter of 1-1/2 years and a son four months old. Albrecht a daughter of four months. Each tried to create independent situations as merchants, and both were unsuccessful. Nearly 1-1/2 years ago Ludwig lost $1500 of his uninsured property in a fire, and I was unable to help re-establish him. Ludwig and Albrecht are with their families luckily healthy and have to see how they get through.

6) Of our dear daughters is Louise (Lula), born 1859, is the oldest. She married the teacher Ernst Langhammer[1] two and one-half years ago and has a one-year-old daughter. She lives happily with her husband who is only two years older than she. Both have at their disposal a good living.

7) Marie born 1861 spent two years as a teaching assistant to her brother, Sigismund at the local school, and since November 1, has taken over an independent school 16 miles from here and earns $300 for eight months in the year.

8) and 9) Valeska and Lina, born respectfully 26 March 1863 and 10 August 1864, our dear youngest daughters, are at home with us and the joy of our old days. They help where and when they can and let no feelings of loneliness come over us. Lina, the youngest, goes in the winter time in addition to five days a week to the school where Sigismund teaches and works with teaching the smaller children. Both girls are very strong.

1 Son of the Valeska Kleberg Langhammer (see note 1 page 109).

Millheim, Texas January 10, 1887

10) Wilhelm and 11) Ferdinand, both youngest sons, show, namely the first, only very moderate intellectual ambition; Ferdinand visits still the school, which Wilhelm quit a year ago. Both play the violin very well and entertain with Marie and Lina good singing and playing guitar, and give us many richly enjoyable hours. The acquisition of good handwork will certainly furnish advancement to both of them the most.

Here have I given you a detailed description of my family and possessions, from the sad to unhappy. But the same is for all, what causes me many sleepless nights, hangs over me as a Damocles[1] sword; it is the disastrous unassessable lot of my son, Fritz, with his many underage children. Every moment can it bring for him and for me. But the thought of the reality is horrifying enough; why should I let my imagination bring more; and yet, I have in a much agitated life always have found that which is needed to get through.

Our domestic life is now neither overladen with many people nor lonely through need of them. We elders, four children, and a grandchild farm the home place. We have remained spared of needing a doctor for many years, which if necessary would be very costly. In addition I have acquired the experience from so many years to perform the necessary things with some strength. Spheres of the daughters are attended mostly by the mother; also I take a part there. They have frequent visitors or visit and I take them by horse and carriage. I myself occasionally visit the bowling alley or push the billiards playing for

1 According to Webster's New World Dictionary, in Greek legend., Damocles was a courtier of ancient Syracuse who talked so much about the happiness of being a king that his own king demonstrated the dangers of a ruler's life by seating him at a banquet table just below a sword hanging by a hair.

beers. Earlier I had more pledged acquaintances with people and a way of thinking, but have departed from these thoughts.

Ernst Kleberg, widowed four years ago when his wife, sister of my wife, who lives 400-500 steps from me and who is three years older than I and so hard of hearing, that I must bring slate and pencil to the conversation, and I visit each other regularly one or two times a week and to avoid the conversation, we play "whist in two"[1]. His still older brother, Robert Kleberg, now in the 81st year, lives with his wife, Rosa (also a sister of my wife) and a large family in westerly Texas, 110 miles from here. You, dear Reuter, will perhaps remember him; he was junior barrister and auxiliary judge as he stood with me in Petershagen in 1831. He married in 1834 and emigrated immediately to Texas. He is one of the few surviving veterans who on April 21, 1836, fought in the Battle of San Jacinto for the independence of Texas against Mexico; he and his wife on the annual celebration of this battle will have a free trip through entire Texas and visited us in early years for 14 days and want to also come again this year. His perception and mental powers are undiminished.

Your photograph we have inspected with active interest. It is remarkable to us how much resemblance is your picture, dear Malvine, to my wife. Cheerful strength and health speak out of it. Reuter's picture shows naturally the lines of age, but when one is 75 years old, one cannot be otherwise. I have only had my picture made with my wife 18 years ago. It turned out badly, and I have not tried since then.

Since the winter of 1830-31 when I suffered a severe

---

1 A form of two-handed bridge, a card game generally played by four people.

lung inflammation in Berlin, I have always had, not a direct weakness, but attacks of bad chest colds. I am of the conviction that had I remained in Germany, I long ago would have died of such an attack. Otherwise, I am healthy, and have through regulated and moderate living habits retained a tenacity and strength that amazes many; I swim 20-30 minutes without pause and without tiring. So then I wish for you, dear Reuter, the many small things that offer pleasures in life at our age remain until our deaths.

As more of our friends are lost through death, the feeling of isolation overcomes us, and so these sometimes unpleasant circumstances naturally happen at our age, and, unfortunately, we can do nothing.

And to you, dear Sister Malvine, I wish you the preservation of your strong health and your fresh spirit. Hearty greetings to both of you from my wife and our children, are with us and enjoy the best of health by God's will. Take care,
Your loving brother,
F. Engelking

Millheim July 20, 1891

Dear Sister Malvine,
I should have written to you long ago and began a letter once, but tore it up because I was in too dreary a mood; now I want to write and describe to you my situation.
I live with my daughter, Lina, and son, Ferdinand, and the little Anna[1] on my farm; our single income is the broomcorn sale; we have with expensive strange help $12 monthly to cultivate the plants. From this compensation we must employ the greatest thriftiness and industry; this year the shoots have not made because of a long drought. Our corn is for the circumstances considerably good, so that we have enough food for ourselves and our cattle.
The roof on my house is very bad; of course, I have no prospect to repair it. I have bequeathed to my son, Ferdinand, and Lina all that I have for they want to remain here when I am here no more.
Ferdinand goes to a school to learn raised writing[2] and is also learning to repair piano keys; he thinks that he can earn something from this later; the instruction costs nothing. Fritz, the second oldest son was again in the mental hospital for five months, and is recovered and returned back to his children. Wilhelm was married on May 5 and is at Hallettsville, 60 miles from here, a small city of 2000 residents, where he manufactures soda water. He should have his means. Valeska married last October 1; her husband has the school to carry and they have their means. My son, Carl, lost his good wife; she left behind ten children of whom the youngest is 14

1 The youngest child of her son, Fritz.
2 Blinded by an accident in his youth, he learned braille.

months; it is bad for him.

I cannot live with any of my married children and neither can Lina nor Ferdinand. Lina could find a home with any of them and Ferdinand could not, but would she be happy is the question. You mentioned in your previous letter that I should give up the authority, and I would be pleased to do so if I could give it up, but there is no one who wants to take it on. I must remain here so long as I can and make a home for Ferdinand and Lina.

I hope you will not take this letter too seriously and will write me a friendly answer as you always have done. With hearty greeting to you and those close to you of your sincere sister
Lina Engelking[1]

---

1 She lived approximately 14 more years.

Index

Albrecht.. 60, 72, 140, 157, 177, 179, 201
Alexandria.................. 195
Amalie 11, 65, 72, 82f., 87, 102, 117, 120, 139, 142f., 147, 149, 153, 155f., 168, 173, 175, 179, 187f., 190f.
Amalie Louise........ 11, 147
America.... 14, 19, 21, 33f., 47, 49, 52f., 56ff., 63, 68f., 72, 85, 91, 110, 120, 127, 129f., 142, 145, 150, 163, 167, 176, 183
American Consul.......... 120
Americans..................... 33
Amsler............... 43, 52
Andalusian..................... 47
Anna..... 162, 170, 187, 207
Annuity........................ 161
Arnold 82, 156, 162, 169f., 175, 187
Auguste.... 11, 21f., 76, 81, 86f., 102, 108f., 114, 162
Aurora..................... 50
Austin 3, 17, 41, 43, 45, 60, 65, 79, 132, 135, 200
Austin County.. 41, 43, 45, 60, 65, 79, 132, 135
Baum 11, 21f., 55, 57, 65f., 72, 76, 79, 81f., 86f., 90, 102, 113, 119, 149, 153, 156, 161, 165, 167, 170, 172, 187
Baumann 11, 21f., 55, 65f., 72, 76, 82, 87, 102, 119, 149, 153, 156, 161, 165, 167, 170, 187
Baumgarten 57, 79, 81, 86, 90, 113
Bavaria........................ 25
Beaumont.................... 196
Bellville............... 199, 201
Benoit.......................... 101
Berlin.......................... 204
Bernau.... 12, 82, 156, 175, 187
Between-deck passengers... 26
Bonn.......................... 159
Bottoms................... 48, 84
Brazos.... 31, 50, 99f., 143, 189
Bremen.. 25f., 56, 58f., 71, 75, 79, 81ff., 85, 91, 103, 109f., 115, 117f., 120, 124, 172
Bremer ship...... 19, 21, 26, 102, 105
Bremerhaven.... 21, 25, 56, 117
Brennholz.................... 151
Bridles........................ 37

193

Bridoon............... 37, 40, 149
Brosig..................... 164
Buchholz................ 135f.
Cabin passenger... 20f., 26, 58, 94, 117
California.................. 181
Carl 11, 20, 26, 87, 97, 119, 173, 177f., 182, 200f., 208
Carl Georg Heinrich....... 11
Carollton.................... 12
Carrollton............. 97, 101
Cat Spring... 41, 43, 45, 60, 65ff., 75, 79, 86, 94, 108, 200
Cattle.... 22, 28, 48, 53, 56, 70, 76, 84f., 90, 98, 100, 109, 136, 175, 178, 188, 190ff., 198, 201, 207
Chamber pot................ 33
Charlotte............... 11, 142
Chocolate................... 33
Christine Charlotte......... 11
Cigar............. 60f., 66, 124
Cincinnati... 126, 128f., 150
Circus Renz......... 168, 170
Cleveland............ 126, 128
Coffee. 32f., 38, 47, 73, 91, 105, 121, 145, 187, 197
Coffeehouse.............. 32f.
Cologne...... 117, 132, 139, 147, 149, 153, 155, 159, 161, 163, 165, 167, 169, 171, 175
Cologne October 19, 1853.

Columbia........ 58, 135, 189
Confederacy............... 197
Congress..................... 51
Coopers Romance........ 143
Cotton... 19, 22, 53, 59, 73, 85, 90, 93, 99f., 178, 182, 197f., 200
Counts from Waldeck and Leiningen-Westerburg ... 81
Cremor Tartori............. 106
Creole....................... 150
Dankenwerth............ 57, 93
Dankwerth.............. 81, 114
Dannemann................. 21
Day laborer............ 56, 182
Deer...................... 19, 22
Delius......... 63, 65f., 69, 71
Delius of Versmold......... 63
Dessau...................... 91
Diarrhea............... 142, 189
Drews....................... 91
Dunkirk.................... 127
Education costs............... **13**
Emilien..................... 168
Engelmann................. 100
England......... 85, 120, 123
Epileptic fit.................. 191
Ervenberg................... 72
Europe.. 29, 32, 46, 48, 59, 70, 73, 85, 107, 120, 123, 140
Farmer 19, 21, 28f., 50, 52, 69, 73, 110f., 182f.

Index

Fayette............ 3, 17
Ferdinand. 1, 12, 14, 20, 23, 26, 35, 37, 60, 63, 74, 77, 79, 87, 90, 93, 95, 101, 103, 108, 114, 116, 119f., 138f., 143, 153, 155, 161, 163, 171, 175, 177, 202, 207f.
Ferdinand Engelking....... 1, 12ff., 20, 23, 26, 35, 37, 60, 63, 74, 77, 79, 87, 90, 93, 95, 101, 103, 108, 114, 116, 119f., 138f., 143, 153, 155, 161, 163, 171, 175, 177, 202, 207f.
Fever........ 46, 65, 92, 97ff., 101ff., 105ff., 142
Fischer and Danzwert..... 50
France............ 85
Franklin............ 163
Fransiska, Ship............ 117
Friederike............ 11, 37, 79
Fritz.......... 172, 175, 177ff., 182f., 197, 199f., 202, 207
Furniture............ 83, 161
Galveston........ 27f., 31, 46, 56ff., 71f., 81ff., 89f., 93, 98ff., 102f., 105f., 109, 112, 123, 129, 143ff., 155, 157, 161, 163, 172, 188f., 191
German 1ff., 17f., 25, 27ff., 32ff., 37f., 40, 48ff., 56, 58, 60, 65ff., 69, 73, 76, 81f., 86, 89, 91ff., 101ff., 108ff., 120, 122, 127, 129, 135f., 149, 176f., 182f., 187f., 191f., 199, 204
German newspaper......... 33
German Texana............ 149
Germany 2f., 18, 25, 29, 32, 34f., 37, 48f., 58, 60, 65f., 73, 76, 81f., 89, 91, 101ff., 109, 120, 129, 177, 187f., 191f., 204
Gilbert Jordan............ 149
Globe, Ship............ 145
Glogau......... 113
Goodeye............ 172
Göttingen............ 156, 167
Graeser............ 71, 82f.
Gulf of Mexico..... 57, 129, 144
Gunpowder............ 38
Hagen............ 12
Halle............ 61
Hallettsville............ 207
Hamburg............ 35
Hammer, a Catholic priest.. 128
Havre............ 60, 139
Hecker............ 59
Heinmann............ 130
Heinsberg.. 130ff., 135, 147
Henriette Friederica Caroline............ 11
Herford............ 72
Hermann............ 61, 91
Heye............ 92, 94
Heymann............ 92

Hollien...... 52, 97, 109, 164
Homeguard................... 197
Houston.. 3, 17, 31, 46, 50, 57f., 66f., 89, 99f., 102f., 108, 114, 143f., 191, 196
Höxter............ 12, 155, 168
Humboldt...................... 163
Hunting.... 19f., 22, 35, 48, 130
Immigrant. 28, 31, 51, 107, 145, 192
Immigrants............. 28, 107
Immigrate... 19, 50, 72, 108
Indian............... 51, 110, 136
Industry 50, 79, 87, 99, 207
Jewish............................ 91
Joseph Hahn................... 27
Julia, ship............ 19, 21, 25
Julie.. 12, 65f., 72, 76, 82f., 87, 119, 153, 156, 162
Julie Marie..................... 12
Julien.... 65f., 72, 82f., 119, 153, 156
Justice of the peace....... 190
Justine Friederike Auguste Bokelmann.................... 11
Kanaster.......................... 60
Kaufmann... 71, 81ff., 103, 105, 112f.
Kleberg 28f., 31, 40, 43, 46, 51f., 59, 61, 69, 72, 76, 81ff., 89f., 97, 102, 108, 140, 143, 154ff., 203
Klein Sandkaul..... 139, 159
Kuhdüngers.................... 84
Lake Erie....................... 128
Langhammer...... 155f., 201
Legros........................... 131
Leiningen.................. 81, 89
Leiningen-Westerburg.... 81
Lina...... 55, 143, 177, 196, 202, 207f.
Liverpool................. 89, 132
Longscope............ 171, 175
Louis 12, 14f., 20, 37, 55f., 59f., 69, 72f., 76, 82f., 87, 91f., 95, 97ff., 108, 129, 147, 195, 201
Louis Ferdinand....... 12, 14
Louis, ship.................... 115
Louisiana........ 12, 179, 195
Ludwig 135, 155, 177, 179, 201
Ludwig Buchholz......... 135
Maetze.......... 140, 155, 177
Malvine.. 12, 19, 87, 204f., 207
Malvine Ferdinande Louise 12
Manncopf...................... 20
Marie............... 12, 177, 202
Maryland............. 179, 193
Max Von Der Decken..... 59
Meals.......... 20, 34, 47, 150
Medicine 56, 101, 103, 107, 197
Mexicans.. 28, 47, 67f., 85f.
Mexico... 57, 68, 85f., 129,

Index

144, 204
Mill Creek......... 31, 50, 68
Millheim..... 144, 172, 177, 187, 189, 196, 207
Mississippi.... 92, 126, 144, 150, 193ff.
Missouri............ 19, 21, 28
Moncy.......... 43
Mosel............. 91
Mother.... 20ff., 25, 27, 32, 37, 43, 45, 54f., 58, 60, 65, 69f., 72f., 75, 77, 79, 81, 89ff., 94, 97, 105, 115, 119f., 167, 169, 178, 203
Muhr............ 172
Mülheim...... 159
Murmann..... 128
Nagel........... 172
Nassau......... 81
Nathan.......... 46
Negress........ 56
Negro.......... 113, 183, 197f.
Neuhaus....... 187
Neuton......... 46
New Orleans.... 19ff., 25ff., 32, 35, 45f., 57f., 63, 65f., 68f., 72, 75f., 79, 81f., 89ff., 97ff., 101ff., 105, 115, 126, 129, 139, 145, 150f., 191
New York.. 35, 123, 126ff., 145, 151, 172
Nolte..... 140, 155, 171, 175
Paderborn 76, 90, 108, 118, 139, 155f., 187
Pecan.... 48, 81, 87, 90, 105
Pecan Grove..... 81, 87, 90, 105
Percussion........ 38
Petershagen........ 204
Ploeger........ 55, 81, 86, 108
Pochhammer........ 159
Potatoes........ 31
Prairie....... 48f., 67, 84, 136
Prospect Hill........ 128, 132
Prussian Cour........ 70
Quartermaster........ 197
Quenzel........ 164
Reuter. 12, 17, 19f., 35, 61, 71, 82, 87, 89f., 119, 153, 156, 177, 181, 187, 203f.
Rhea........ 19
Rhine Inn........ 139
Rhineland........ 128
Richmond........ 193f.
Rifle........ 19, 22, 38
Rio Grande........ 85
Roeder 1f., 28, 46, 52f., 60, 67, 72, 75, 86, 108, 113
Roger and Formes........ 170
Rosa........ 46, 72, 199, 203
Rotterdam........ 139
Rudolph Engelking..... 119, 185
Säccolet........ 172
Sack 40f., 55, 70f., 81, 102, 108, 113f.
San Antonio........ 67, 85

San Felipe. 31, 75, 99, 108, 143, 189, 199f.
San Jacinto................... 204
Sarrazin....................... 108
Scheinbridge................ 159
Schieffer..... 11, 66, 71, 87, 102, 112, 117, 120, 132, 136, 141, 147, 154, 157, 177, 181, 187ff., 198
Schildesche..................... 12
Schlüsselburg 11ff., 19, 37, 40, 45, 63, 76, 79, 91, 97, 101, 105, 115, 119, 139, 153, 155, 165
Schmidt.. 65f., 68f., 81, 89, 92
Schneider....................... 164
Sealy.................... 119, 185
Seasickness..... 25, 56, 119, 123
Shackelford..................... 89
Sharpsburg..................... 193
Shop. 34, 72, 91, 182, 192, 199
Sigismund 172, 177, 193ff., 199f., 202
Silesia............................. 70
Slavery..................... 3, 17
Sophie Christine Auguste... 11
South Confederation..... 192
South Hampton............. 123
Southeastern Seacoast.... 28
Spanish doubloons... 26, 58

Spanish horse................. 58
St. Louis......... 20, 91f., 98, 100ff., 129
Stängo............................ 172
Steamboat......... 31, 57, 129
Steamer....... 126, 132, 139, 143ff., 189, 195
Steamer Arthur............. 144
Steamer Farmer............ 144
Steamer Mexico........... 144
Steamship... 27, 31, 46, 92, 99f., 102, 123, 143, 150, 163, 189, 193
Steamship City of Glasgow 163
Steamship Franklin....... 163
Steamship Humbold..... 163
Stirrups.................... 37, 40
Stolzenau........... 37, 57, 79
Straten........................... 159
Swearingen................... 132
Tea................ 33, 47, 195
Teacher... 28, 86, 117, 156, 177, 199, 201
Tennessee......... 19, 21, 195
Tewes....................... 91f.
Texas 3, 17, 28f., 31f., 34f., 41, 45f., 50, 58, 60, 63, 65, 67, 69, 71, 73, 75, 79, 81, 85f., 90, 92f., 98, 101, 113f., 118ff., 130f., 135f., 142, 145, 163, 167, 172, 175, 177f., 181f., 185, 187ff., 193, 199, 203f.

Index

Theater.... 27, 33, 159, 170, 193
Thönneshen................ 131ff.
Tobacco.. 19f., 22, 60, 65f., 70, 85, 90, 94, 100, 105, 109, 112, 121, 127
Triest............................ 92
Tuscaloosa..................... 50
United States.... 28, 47, 81, 97, 136
University... 3, 13f., 17, 149
Valesca......................... 136
Valeska. 155, 177, 202, 208
Velhegen........................ 61
Verden........................... 91
Versmold.................. 63, 65
Vienna........................... 91
Virginia................. 179, 193
Von Roeder 1f., 28, 46, 60, 67, 72, 75, 86, 108, 113
Wages........................... 22
Waldeck......................... 81
Walter Scott................. 143
Washeberg................... 160
Washington.................. 135
Washington County...... 182
Washington. ship.......... 123
Weevil................ 178f., 182
Wennmahr.................... 156
Wennock....................... 140
Wilhelm.. 12, 63, 177, 202, 207
Wilms swindle............. 175
Windheim................. 63, 75
Wine... 32, 48, 58, 91, 119, 132, 142, 145, 171, 187
Wolff........................... 172
Yankee................ 193f., 198
Yellow fever.. 46, 92, 97ff., 101f., 106f.
Zieserock..................... 113
.... 147

www.ingramcontent.com/pod-product-compliance
Lightning Source LLC
LaVergne TN
LVHW092006090526
838202LV00001B/21